C O L E S

Getting Along in . . .

Spanish

For travellers and students

Useful phrases with pronunciations

Travel & culture tips

ABOUT COLES NOTES

COLES NOTES have been an indispensable aid to students on five continents since 1948.

COLES NOTES now offer titles on a wide range of general interest topics as well as traditional academic subject areas and individual literary works. All COLES NOTES are written by experts in their fields and reviewed for accuracy by independent authorities and the Coles Editorial Board.

COLES NOTES provide clear, concise explanations of their subject areas. Proper use of COLES NOTES will result in a broader understanding of the topic being studied. For academic subjects, Coles Notes are an invaluable aid for study, review and exam preparation. For literary works, COLES NOTES provide interesting interpretations and evaluations which supplement the text but are not intended as a substitute for reading the text itself. Use of the NOTES will serve not only to clarify the material being studied, but should enhance the reader's enjoyment of the topic.

COLES PUBLISHING. A division of Prospero Books
Toronto - Canada
Printed in Canada

Cataloguing in Publication Data
Berg, Gordon, 1942-

Coles Notes: Getting along in ... Spanish

ISBN 0-7740-0572-6

1. Spanish language - Conversation and phrase books. 2. Spanish language - Textbooks for second language learners - English speakers.* I. Title II. Series

PC4129.E5B47 1998 448.3'421 C97-932599-4

Publisher: Nigel Berrisford
Editing by Paul Kropp Communications
Book design and layout by Karen Petherick, Markham, Ontario

Manufactured by Webcom Limited
Cover finish: Webcom's Exclusive DURACOAT

Contents

Getting Along in Spanish
Introduction

Getting Along in Spanish is a Spanish phrase book and survival guide that is designed to be helpful to travellers to Spain, Mexico and Latin America who have a limited familiarity with Spanish. The book will also be useful to students enrolled in beginning courses in conversational Spanish.

The guide begins with an easy-to-understand pronunciation guide to the language, noting the major differences between American (Am) and standard Spanish (Sp) pronunciations. It is followed by a preliminary chapter that deals with "need-to-know" words and expressions: greetings, numbers, days and dates, money, telling time, weather expressions and question words.

The remaining material in this guide is organized by themes (e.g., at the airport, at the hotel, dining out...) and provides information and handy phrases that will be useful to both novice and experienced travellers.

If you really want to enjoy your travels in Spanish-speaking countries, there are a few essential rules that you should establish for yourself. Number one on the list is flexibility. Remember, you're not in Canada, so learn to be patient. The notorious "Mexican minute" and splendid Spanish siesta make good sense in those countries. Secondly, maintain a sense of humor. Travel is full of minor annoyances, from **turista** to terrible tacos, but don't let little things get you down. Finally, respect the Spanish people and the differences of their culture. Open your arms and your mind and embrace this new adventure. The entire Spanish-speaking world awaits you.

Keep in mind that Spanish-speaking people are generally friendly and hospitable. They are patient and appreciate tourists who make an attempt to communicate in their language. You may have certainly heard the phrase **Mi casa es su casa** - "My house is your house." What warmer welcome could you possibly expect?

Spanish in a nutshell

Here's a list of the most basic expressions in Spanish, well worth memorizing on your plane flight.

Good morning.	Buenos días.	**bweh**-nohs **dee**-ahs
Good afternoon.	Buenas tardes.	**bweh**-nahs **tahr**-dehs
Hi!	¡Hola!	**oh**-lah
Bye.	Adiós.	ah-**dyohs**
Yes/No.	Sí/No.	see/noh
Excuse me.	Perdón.	pehr-**dohn**
Please.	Por favor.	pohr fah-**bohr**
Thank you.	Gracias.	**grah**-syahs (Latin America) **grah**-thyahs (Spain)
I don't understand.	No comprendo.	noh kohm-**prehn**-doh
Do you speak English?	¿Habla usted inglés?	**ah**-blah oo-**stehd** een-**glehs**
I'm Canadian.	Soy canadiense.	soy kah-nah-**dyehn**-seh
Where is...?	¿Dónde está...?	**dohn**-deh eh-**stah**
I'd like to buy...	Quisiera comprar...	kee-**syeh**-rah kohm-**prahr**
How much does it cost?	¿Cuánto cuesta?	**kwahn**-toh **kweh**-stah

Then add a smile and some effective finger pointing. This quick list might get you through your first few hours in a Spanish-speaking country.

CHAPTER ONE

Pronunciation Chart

Spanish is a fairly easy language for English speakers to pronounce. Unlike much of English and some other Romance languages, Spanish is a phonetic language. Simply pronounce everything that you see with the exception of the letter "h" which is silent. This guide provides a phonetic transcription for each phrase that will be easy for English speakers to follow. However, by following a few rules concerning Spanish pronunciation, you will soon find that you can pronounce the phrases by reading the actual Spanish text.

The stressed syllable in each transcribed word throughout this guide is indicated in boldface print. Where pronunciations differ, the Castillian Spanish of Spain is marked (Sp) and the Spanish of Mexico and Latin America is marked (Am).

Vowels

a	as in "father"	ah	casa	**kah**-sah
e	as in "date"	eh	fecha	**feh**-chah
i	as in "see"	ee	libro	**lee**-broh
o	as in "no"	oh	como	**koh**-moh
u	as in "fluid"	oo	lunes	**loo**-nehs

Vowel Combinations (Dipthongs)

au	as in "cow"	ow	auto	**ow**-toh
ai/ay	as in "eye"	ahy	baile	**bahy**-leh
			hay	ahy
ei	as in "say"	ay	treinta	**trayn**-tah
oi/oy	as in "boy"	oy	oigo	**oy**-goh
			estoy	eh-**stoy**
ia	as in "yard"	yah	viaje	**byah**-heh
ie	as in "yes"	yeh	siete	**syeh**-teh
io/yo	as in "yoyo"	yoh	miope	**myoh**-peh
			mayo	**mah**-yoh
iu	as in "fuel"	yoo	viuda	**byoo**-dah
ua	as in "water"	wah	agua	**ah**-gwah
ue	as in "way"	weh	bueno	**bweh**-noh
uo	as in "woe"	woh	antiguo	ahn-**tee**-gwoh
ui	as in "we"	wee	Luis	lwees

Consonants

The following consonants have sounds similar to English: **b, d, f, k, l, m, n, p, s and t.**

c (before e/i)	as in "see"	s (Am)	cena	**seh**-nah
			cine	**see**-neh
	as in "both"	th (Sp)	cena	**theh**-nah
			cine	**thee**-neh
c (before anything else)				
	as in "keep"	k	cama	**kah**-mah
			como	**koh**-moh
			cuando	**kwahn**-doh
			claro	**klah**-roh

ch	as in "chin"		chico	**chee**-koh
g (before e/i)	as in "help"	h	general	heh-neh-**rahl**
			gitano	hee-**tah**-noh
g (before anything else)				
	as in "go"	g	gato	**gah**-toh
			goma	**goh**-mah
h	always silent		hablar	ah-**blahr**
j	as in "help"	h	José	hoh-**seh**
ll	as in "yes"	y (Am)	Castilla	kah-**stee**-yah
	as in "million	ly (Sp)	Castilla	kah-**stee**-lyah
ñ	as in "canyon"	ny	señora	seh-**nyoh**-rah
qu	as in "keep"	k	quedar	keh-**dahr**
			química	**kee**-mee-kah
r	trilled once	r	pero	**peh**-roh
rr (+ initial r)	trilled twice	rr	perro	**peh**-rroh
			rico	**rree**-koh
v	same as "b"	b	vivir	bee-**beer**
x (before a vowel)				
	as in "locks"	ks	examen	ehk-**sah**-mehn
x (before a consonant)				
	as in "locks"	ks (Am)	extra	**ehk**-strah
	as in "see"	s (Sp)	extra	**eh**-strah
z	as in "see"	s (Am)	zona	**soh**-nah
	as in "both"	th (Sp)	zona	**thoh**-nah

A little punctuation . . .

Questions in written Spanish have an inverted question mark before the phrase and the regular question mark after.

How are you? ¿Cómo está usted? **koh**-moh eh-**stah** oo-**stehd**

Exclamation marks work the same way.

Hi! ¡Hola! **oh**-lah

There are two simple rules to follow in order to emphasize the right syllable in Spanish:

1. If a word ends in a vowel, an "n" or an "s," stress the second to last syllable.

muchacho	moo-**chah**-choh
necesitan	neh-seh-**see**-tahn (Am)
	neh-theh-**see**-tahn (Sp)
billetes	bee-**yeh**-tehs (Am)
	bee-**lyeh**-tehs (Sp)

2. If a word ends in anything else, stress the last syllable.

color	koh-**lohr**
español	eh-spah-**nyohl**

Any word that breaks these rules will require a written accent over the stressed vowel.

capitán	kah-pee-**tahn**
lápiz	**lah**-pees (Am)
	lah-peeth (Sp)
difícil	dee-**fee**-seel (Am)
	dee-**fee**-theel (Sp)

In addition, all question words have accent marks over the stressed vowel.

¿Cómo?	**koh**-moh
¿Quién?	kyehn
¿Cuánto?	**kwahn**-toh
¿Dónde?	**dohn**-deh

CHAPTER TWO

The Basics

GREETINGS AND EXPRESSIONS OF COURTESY

Knowing a few basic greetings and expressions of courtesy will go a long way in paving the road to meaningful conversation. Even though some of the people you meet may speak English, they will certainly appreciate the effort that you make to speak their language.

Good morning.	Buenos días.	**bweh**-nohs **dee**-ahs
Good afternoon.	Buenas tardes.	**bweh**-nahs **tahr**-dehs
Good evening/night.	Buenas noches.	**bweh**-nahs **noh**-chehs

Buenas noches is normally used after 6:00 p.m.

Hi!	¡Hola!	**oh**-lah
How are you?	¿Cómo está usted?	**koh**-moh eh-**stah** oo-**stehd**
How's everything?	¿Qué tal?	keh tahl
What's new?	¿Qué hay de nuevo?	keh ahy deh **nweh**-boh
Fine, thanks.	Bien, gracias.	byehn **grah**-syahs (Am)
		byehn **grah**-thyahs (Sp)
And you?	¿Y usted?	ee oo-**stehd**
So, so.	Así, así.	ah-**see** ah-**see**
OK.	Regular.	rreh-goo-**lahr**
Not very well.	No muy bien.	noh mwee byehn
Goodbye.	Adiós.	ah-**dyohs**
See you later.	Hasta luego.	**ah**-stah **lweh**-goh
	Hasta la vista.	**ah**-stah lah **bee**-stah
See you soon.	Hasta pronto.	**ah**-stah **prohn**-toh
See you tomorrow.	Hasta mañana.	**ah**-stah mah-**nyah**-nah

What's your name?	¿Cómo se llama usted?	**koh**-moh seh **yah**-mah oo-**stehd** (Am)
		koh-moh seh **lyah**-mah oo-**stehd** (Sp)
My name is ...	Me llamo ...	me **yah**-moh (Am)
		me **lyah**-moh (Sp)
Do you speak English?	¿Habla usted inglés?	**ah**-blah oo-**stehd** een-**glehs**
I'm Canadian.	Soy canadiense.	soy kah-nah-**dyehn**-seh
I'm a tourist.	Soy turista.	soy too-**ree**-stah
Excuse me.	Perdón.	pehr-**dohn**
I don't understand.	No comprendo.	noh kohm-**prehn**-doh
Please.	Por favor.	pohr fah-**bohr**
Slower, please.	Más despacio, por favor.	mahs deh-**spah**-syoh pohr fah-**bohr** (Am)
		mahs deh-**spah**-thyoh pohr fah-**bohr** (Sp)
Please repeat.	Repita, por favor.	rreh-**pee**-tah pohr fah-**bohr**
Could you write that down, please?	¿Podría escribirlo, por favor?	poh-**dree**-ah eh-skree-**beer**-loh pohr fah-**bohr**
Thank you very much.	Muchas gracias.	**moo**-chahs **grah**-syahs (Am)
		moo-chahs **grah**-thyahs (Sp)
You're welcome.	De nada.	deh **nah**-dah

QUESTION WORDS

Who?	¿Quién? (singular)	kyehn
	¿Quiénes? (plural)	**kyeh**-nehs
What?	¿Qué?	keh
Which (one)?	¿Cuál?	kwahl
Which (ones)?	¿Cuáles?	**kwah**-lehs
Where?	¿Dónde?	**dohn**-deh
From where?	¿De dónde?	deh **dohn-**deh
To where?	¿Adónde?	ah-**dohn**-deh
When?	¿Cuándo?	**kwahn**-doh
Why?	¿Por qué?	pohr-**keh**
How?	¿Cómo?	**koh**-moh
How much?	¿Cuánto (a)?	**kwahn**-toh (tah)
How many?	¿Cuántos (as)?	**kwahn**-tohs (tahs)

Notice that all question words in Spanish have a written accent. Written questions in Spanish begin with an inverted question mark and end with a normal question mark.

When you haven't heard something clearly or you want something repeated, people often say "What?" in English. In Spanish, this phrase is rendered by **¿Cómo? (koh**-moh). Our all-purpose Canadian "eh?" means **hey!** or **hi!** in Spanish, so temptation to use it should probably be resisted.

NUMBERS

As travellers, you will be required to use numbers immediately upon your arrival to explain to customs officials the duration of your stay. A knowledge of numbers will also assist you when exchanging money, making purchases, paying bills, making phone calls, determining the price of cabs and seeking addresses. The Spanish numbering system is fairly easy.

Cardinal Numbers

Cardinal numbers are used for quantity, in addresses and in dates in Spanish.

1	uno	**oo**-noh
2	dos	dohs
3	tres	trehs
4	cuatro	**kwah**-troh
5	cinco	**seen**-koh (Am)
		theen-koh (Sp)
6	seis	**say**-ees
7	siete	**syeh**-teh
8	ocho	**oh**-choh
9	nueve	**nweh**-beh
10	diez	dyehs (Am)
		dyehth (Sp)

11	once	**ohn**-seh (Am)
		ohn-theh (Sp)
12	doce	**doh**-seh (Am)
		doh-theh (Sp)
13	trece	**treh**-seh (Am)
		treh-theh (Sp)
14	catorce	kah-**tohr**-seh (Am)
		kah-**tohr**-theh (Sp)
15	quince	**keen**-seh (Am)
		keen-theh (Sp)
16	dieciséis	dyeh-see-**says** (Am)
		dyeh-thee-**says** (Sp)
17	diecisiete	dyeh-see-**syeh**-teh (Am)
		dyeh-thee-**syeh**-teh (Sp)
18	dieciocho	dyeh-**syoh**-choh (Am
		dyeh-**thyoh**-choh (Sp)
19	diecinueve	dyeh-see-**nweh**-beh (Am)
		dyeh-thee-**nweh**-beh (Sp)
20	veinte	**bayn**-teh
21	veintiuno	bayn-**tyoo**-noh
22	veintidós	bayn-tee-**dohs**
23	veintitrés	bayn-tee-**trehs**
24	veinticuatro	bayn-tee-**kwah**-troh
30	treinta	**trayn**-tah
31	treinta y uno	trayn-tahy-**oo**-noh
35	treinta y cinco	trayn-tahy-**seen**-koh (Am)
		trayn-tahy-**theen**-koh (Sp)
40	cuarenta	kwah-**rehn**-tah
41	cuarenta y uno	kwah-rehn-tahy-**oo**-noh
50	cincuenta	seen-**kwehn**-tah (Am)
		theen-**kwehn**-tah (Sp)
51	cincuenta y uno	seen-kwehn-tahy-**oo**-noh (Am)
		theen-kwehn-tahy-**oo**-noh (Sp)
60	sesenta	seh-**sehn**-tah
61	sesenta y uno	seh-sehn-tahy-**oo**-noh
70	setenta	seh-tehn-tah
71	setenta y uno	seh-tehn-tahy-**oo**-noh
80	ochenta	oh-**chehn**-tah

90	noventa	noh-**behn**-tah
100	cien	syehn (Am)
		thyehn (Sp)
101	ciento uno	syehn-toh **oo**-noh (Am)
		thyehn-toh **oo**-noh (Sp)
200	doscientos (as)	dohs-**syehn**-tohs (tahs) (Am)
		dohs-**thyehn**-tohs (tahs) (Sp)
300	trescientos (as)	trehs-**syehn**-tohs (tahs) (Am)
		trehs-**thyehn**-tohs (tahs) (Sp)
400	cuatrocientos (as)	kwah-troh-**syehn**-tohs (tahs) (Am)
		kwah-troh-**thyehn**-tohs (tahs) (Sp)
500	quinientos (as)	kee-**nyehn**-tohs (tahs)
600	seiscientos (as)	says-**syehn**-tohs (tahs) (Am)
		says-**thyehn**-tohs (tahs) (Sp)
700	setecientos (as)	seh-teh-**syehn**-tohs (tahs) (Am)
		seh-teh-**thyehn**-tohs (tahs) (Sp)
800	ochocientos (as)	oh-choh-**syehn**-tohs (tahs) (Am)
		oh-choh-**thyehn**-tohs (tahs) (Sp)
900	novecientos (as)	noh-beh-**syehn**-tohs (tahs) (Am)
		noh-beh-**thyehn**-tohs (tahs) (Sp)
1,000	mil	meel
2,000	dos mil	dohs meel

The numbers 200 to 900 have two forms, one masculine and one feminine. If you're describing males or masculine objects, use the form ending in "os." If the persons or objects you're describing are feminine, then you'll use the form ending in "as."

200 men	doscientos hombres
200 women	doscientas mujeres
300 pesos	trescientos pesos
300 pesetas	trescientas pesetas
500 boys	quinientos chicos
500 girls	quinientas chicas

Ordinal Numbers

Ordinal numbers deal with sequencing, the order in which things occur. They are used to identify the different floors in hotels and department stores.

1st	primero (a)	pree-**meh**-roh (rah)
	primer	pree-**mehr**
2nd	segundo (a)	seh-**goon**-doh (dah)
3rd	tercero (a)	tehr-**seh**-roh (rah) (Am)
		tehr-**theh**-roh (rah) (Sp)
	tercer	tehr-**sehr** (Am)
		tehr-**thehr** (Sp)
4th	cuarto (a)	**kwahr**-toh (tah)
5th	quinto (a)	**keen**-toh (tah)
6th	sexto (a)	**sehk**-stoh (stah) (Am)
		seh-stoh (stah) (Sp)
7th	séptimo (a)	**sehp**-tee-moh (mah)
8th	octavo (a)	ohk-**tah**-boh (bah)
9th	noveno (a)	noh-**beh**-noh (nah)
10th	décimo (a)	**deh**-see-moh (mah) (Am)
		deh-thee-moh (mah) (Sp)

Note that the ground floor in most public buildings is not referred to as the first floor but rather ***la planta baja.*** The second floor would be ***la primera planta***, the third floor would be ***la segunda planta***, etc.

DAYS OF THE WEEK

Today is...	*Hoy es...*	*oy ehs*
Monday	lunes	**loo**-nehs
Tuesday	martes	**mahr**-tehs
Wednesday	miércoles	**myehr**-koh-lehs
Thursday	jueves	**hweh**-behs
Friday		viernes **byehr**-nehs
Saturday	sábado	**sah**-bah-doh
Sunday	domingo	doh-**meen**-goh

Note that days of the week are not capitalized in standard Spanish. However, in Mexico and other Latin American countries, it is common practice to capitalize the days.

DATES

January 1st	el primero de enero	ehl pree-**meh**-roh deh eh-**neh**-roh
February 2nd	el dos de febrero	ehl dohs deh feh-**breh**-roh
March 3rd	el tres de marzo	ehl trehs deh **mahr**-soh (Am)
		ehl trehs deh **mahr**-thoh (Sp)
April 4th	el cuatro de abril	ehl **kwah**-troh deh ah-**breel**
May 5th	el cinco de mayo	ehl **seen**-koh deh **mah**-yoh (Am)
		ehl **theen**-koh deh **mah**-yoh (Sp)
June 6th	el seis de junio	ehl says deh **hoo**-nyoh
July 7th	el siete de julio	ehl **syeh**-teh deh **hoo**-lyoh
August 8th	el ocho de agosto	ehl **oh**-choh deh ah-**goh**-stoh
September 9th	el nueve de septiembre	ehl **nweh**-beh deh sehp-**tyehm**-breh
October 10th	el diez de octubre	ehl dyehs deh ohk-**too**-breh (Am)
		ehl dyehth deh ohk-**too**-breh (Sp)
November 15th	el quince de noviembre	ehl **keen**-seh deh noh-**byehm**-breh (Am)
		ehl **keen**-theh deh noh-**byehm**-breh (Sp)
December 30th	el treinta de diciembre	ehl **trayn**-tah deh dee-**syehm**-breh (Am)
		ehl **trayn**-tah deh dee-**thyehm**-breh (Sp)

SEASONS

Summer	el verano	ehl beh-**rah**-noh
Fall	el otoño	ehl oh-**toh**-nyoh
Winter	el invierno	ehl eem-**byehr**-noh
Spring	la primavera	lah pree-mah-**beh**-rah

Seasons of the year are reversed south of the equator. The summer months are December, January and February; the fall months are March, April and May; the winter months are June, July and August; the spring months are September, October and November. In many of the Atlantic and Pacific resorts south of the equator, Christmas is spent on the beach.

TELLING TIME

You will normally hear and use a 12-hour system when telling time in Spanish. Morning time expressions would be followed by de la mañana [deh lah mah-**nyah**-nah] (a.m.). Afternoon and evening time expressions would be followed by de la tarde [deh lah **tahr**-deh] (p.m.) and de la noche [deh lah **noh**-cheh] (p.m.). Begin using de la noche at 6:00 p.m.

In Mexico, you will commonly hear **en la mañana, en la tarde** and **en la noche**. In some Latin American countries you will also hear **a la mañana, a la tarde** and **a la noche**.

What time is it?	¿Qué hora es?	keh **oh**-rah ehs

There are two ways to express "It is" when telling time in Spanish. Use **Es** with one o'clock, noon and midnight. From two o'clock on, use **Son** to express "It is."

It's...	*Es...*	*ehs*
one o'clock	la una	lah **oo**-nah
five after one	la una y cinco	lah **oo**-nah ee **seen**-koh (Am) lah **oo**-nah ee **theen**-koh (Sp)
one fifteen	la una y cuarto	lah **oo**-nah ee **kwahr**-toh
one thirty	la una y media	lah **oo**-nah ee **meh**-dyah

noon	mediodía	meh-dyoh-**dee**-ah
midnight	medianoche	meh-dyah-**noh**-cheh
It's...	*Son...*	*sohn*
two o'clock	las dos	lahs dohs
two twenty	las dos y veinte	lahs dohs ee **bayn**-teh
two thirty	las dos y media	lahs dohs ee **meh**-dyah
two forty	las tres menos veinte	lahs trehs **meh**-nohs **bayn**-teh
three o'clock	las tres	lahs trehs
four o'clock	las cuatro	lahs **kwah**-troh
four forty-five	las cinco menos cuarto	lahs **seen**-koh **meh**-nohs **kwahr**-toh (Am) lahs **theen**-koh **meh**-nohs **kwahr**-toh (Sp)
five o'clock	las cinco	lahs **seen**-koh (Am) lahs **theen**-koh (Sp)
six o'clock	las seis	lahs says
seven o'clock	las siete	lahs **syeh**-teh
eight o'clock	las ocho	lahs **oh**-choh
nine o'clock	las nueve	lahs **nweh**-beh
ten o'clock	las diez	lahs dyehs (Am) lahs dyehth (Sp)
eleven o'clock	las once	lahs **ohn**-seh (Am) lahs **ohn**-theh (Sp)

After the half hour, minutes are subtracted from the approaching hour. Therefore, **two-forty** would be **three minus twenty** (similar to the English, **twenty to three**).

In Mexico, **two-forty** would be expressed as:

veinte para las tres	**bayn**-teh **pah**-rah lahs trehs

Ten-fifty would be expressed as:

diez para las once	dyehs **pah**-rah lahs **ohn**-seh

(At) what time?	¿A qué hora?	ah keh **oh**-rah
At...	*A...*	*ah*
one o'clock	la una	lah **oo**-nah
noon	mediodía	meh-dyoh-**dee**-ah
ten fifty	las once menos diez	lahs **ohn**-seh **meh**-nohs dyehs (Am) lahs **ohn**-theh **meh**-nohs dyehth (Sp)

The 24-hour system

A 24-hour system is used for bus, train and flight schedules, as well as cinema and theatre times. Simply add 12 to afternoon and evening times. Therefore, 1:00 p.m. would be 13:00, 4:00 p.m. would be 16:00, 8:00 p.m. would be 20:00 and so on up to 12:00 midnight which, in the 24-hour system, would be either 24:00 or 00:00.

5:00 a.m.	05:00	las cinco	lahs **seen**-koh (Am) lahs **theen**-koh (Sp)
10:00 a.m.	10:00	las diez	lahs dyehs (Am) lahs dyehth (Sp)
12:00 noon	12:00	las doce	lahs **doh**-seh (Am) lahs **doh**-theh (Sp)
1:00 p.m.	13:00	las trece	lahs **treh**-seh (Am) lahs **treh**-theh (Sp)
3:15 p.m.	15:15	las quince y quince	lahs **keen**-seh ee **keen**-seh (Am) lahs **keen**-theh ee **keen**-theh (Sp)
12:00 midnight	24:00	las veinticuatro	lahs bayn-tee-**kwah**-troh

MONEY AND BANKING

Although your hotel will exchange traveller's cheques for cash, the best rates are to be found in banks. In many Spanish-speaking countries, banks are open from 8:30 or 9:00 a.m. on weekdays as well as on Saturdays. In Mexico and Spain, there are small currency exchange shops (kiosks), with good exchange rates, that are faster than many banks. Closing times can change according to the season.

If you choose to use an ATM, check with your bank before leaving to make sure that your card will work in foreign machines.

If you have Internet access, you can check daily foreign exchange rates against the Canadian or the American dollar. Simply call up one of your search engines and do a search on "foreign exchange rates."

Here are the monetary units of several Spanish-speaking countries:

Argentina	peso	**peh**-soh
Bolivia	boliviano	boh-lee-**byah**-noh
Chile	peso	**peh**-soh
Colombia	peso	**peh**-soh
Costa Rica	colón	koh-**lohn**
Cuba	peso	**peh**-soh
Ecuador	sucre	**soo**-kreh
España (Spain)	peseta	peh-**seh**-tah
Guatemala	quetzal	keht-**sahl** (Am) keht-**thahl** (Sp)
Honduras	lempira	lehm-**pee**-rah
México	peso	**peh**-soh
Nicaragua	nuevo córdoba	**nweh**-boh **kohr**-doh-bah
Panamá	balboa	bahl-**boh**-ah
Paraguay	guaraní	gwah-rah-**nee**
Perú	sol	sohl
República Dominicana (la)	peso	**peh**-soh
Salvador (el)	colón	koh-**lohn**
Uruguay	peso	**peh**-soh
Venezuela	bolívar	boh-**lee**-bahr

Where is there a bank?	¿Dónde hay un banco?	**dohn**-deh ahy oon **bahn**-koh
Is there a bank nearby?	¿Hay un banco cerca?	ahy oon **bahn**-koh **sehr**-kah (Am) ahy oon **bahn**-koh **thehr**-kah (Sp)
Where is there an ATM?	¿Dónde hay un cajero automático?	**dohn**-deh ahy oon kah-**heh**-roh ow-toh-**mah**-tee-koh
I want to exchange money.	Quiero cambiar dinero.	**kyeh**-roh kahm-**byahr** dee-**neh**-roh
I want to cash traveller's cheques.	Quiero cobrar cheques de viajero.	**kyeh**-roh koh-**brahr** **cheh**-kehs deh byah-**heh**-roh
I want large bills.	Quiero billetes grandes.	**kyeh**-roh bee-**yeh**-tehs **grahn**-dehs (Am) **kyeh**-roh bee-**lyeh**-tehs **grahn**-dehs (Sp)
I want small bills.	Quiero billetes chicos.	**kyeh**-roh bee-**yeh**-tehs **chee**-kohs (Am) **kyeh**-roh bee-**lyeh**-tehs **chee**-kohs (Sp)
I need some change.	Necesito unas monedas.	neh-seh-**see**-toh **oo**-nahs moh-**neh**-dahs (Am) neh-theh-**see**-toh **oo**-nahs moh-**neh**-dahs (Sp)
I would like the change in coins.	Quisiera el cambio en monedas.	kee-**syeh**-rah ehl **kahm**-byoh ehn moh-**neh**-dahs
I don't have any money.	No tengo dinero.	noh **tehn**-goh dee-**neh**-roh
I want to pay with my credit card.	Quisiera pagar con mi tarjeta de crédito.	kee-**syeh**-rah pah-**gahr** kohn mee tahr-**heh**-tah deh **kreh**-dee-toh

Do you accept credit cards?	¿Acepta tarjetas de crédito?	ah-**sehp**-tah tahr-**heh**-tahs deh **kreh**-dee-toh (Am) ah-**thehp**-tah tahr-**heh**-tahs deh **kreh**-dee-toh (Sp)
Can (May) I cash a personal cheque?	¿Puedo cambiar un cheque personal?	**pweh**-doh kahm-**byahr** oon **cheh**-keh pehr-soh-**nahl**
Where should I sign the traveller's cheque?	¿Dónde debo firmar el cheque de viajero?	**dohn**-deh **deh**-boh feer-**mahr** ehl **cheh**-keh deh byah-**heh**-roh
How much is the Canadian dollar worth?	¿A cómo está el dólar canadiense?	ah **koh**-moh eh-**stah** ehl **doh**-lahr kah-nah-**dyehn**-seh
How much is the American dollar worth?	¿A cómo está el dólar americano?	ah **koh**-moh eh-**stah** ehl **doh**-lahr ah-meh-ree-**kah**-noh

Canadian travellers going to major cities should purchase traveller's cheques in Canadian, not American funds, in order to avoid additional charges for converting their money. If you have cheques left over at the end of your trip, you'll also avoid the charges to convert your money back to Canadian funds. But if you're travelling to small towns or many Latin American countries, American traveller's cheques will be easier to cash.

WEATHER EXPRESSIONS

What's the weather like today?	¿Qué tiempo hace hoy?	keh **tyehm**-poh **ah**-seh oy (Am)
		key **tyehm**-poh **ah**-theh oy (Sp)
Is it raining?	¿Llueve?	**yweh**-beh (Am)
		lyweh-beh (Sp)
Is it snowing?	¿Nieva?	**nyeh**-bah
Is it cloudy?	¿Está nublado?	eh-**stah** noo-**blah**-doh
Is it...?	*¿Hace...?*	***ah**-seh (Am)*
		***ah**-theh (Sp)*
nice out	buen tiempo	bwehn **tyehm**-poh
bad out	mal tiempo	mahl **tyehm**-poh
sunny	sol	sohl
hot	calor	kah-**lohr**
cold	frío	**free**-oh
cool	fresco	**freh**-skoh
windy	viento	**byehn**-toh

CHAPTER THREE

Getting started

Canadians travelling abroad require a valid, up-to-date Canadian passport. Your passport is the only proof of citizenship and identity that is universally accepted. It's required upon leaving Canada and upon entering a foreign country. It may also be required when registering in hotels, making business transactions and cashing traveller's cheques. Some hotels ask you to surrender your passport upon registration. Ordinarily, you'll get it back within a few hours, or a day at the most.

APPLYING FOR A PASSPORT

Passport applications are available from all Canadian passport offices and most travel agencies. Please note, Form A is for persons 16 years of age and older. Form B is for persons under the age of 16. Fill out the form carefully and make sure that you include all the necessary support documents requested.

You may apply for your passport either in person or by mail. Applying in person is much faster, since your passport will be ready within five working days. However, you may experience long line-ups when applying in person. If you are in a rush, the Passport Office recommends that you apply on off-days (Wednesdays and Thursdays) and during slower time periods (from opening until 11:00 a.m.) If you apply by mail, you will have to wait two to three weeks before receiving your passport. Payment may be made in cash or by certified cheque or money order.

Mailed applications should be sent to:

The Passport Office
Department of Foreign Affairs and International Trade
Ottawa, ON K1A 0G3

Take the following precautions:

- Make two copies of the identification page of your passport. Leave one copy with a friend or relative and take the other copy with you on your travels (keep it separate from your passport).
- Always keep your passport secure. Keep it protected in a money belt, a shoulder belt or an inside pocket. Pay special attention when going to the beach. It's probably a good idea to leave your passport in the hotel safe unless you have to cash traveller's cheques.
- If you lose your passport, report the loss to the local police and immediately contact the Canadian Embassy or Consulate. Your copy of the identification page of your passport will assist the Canadian officials in issuing you with a replacement passport.

VISA INFORMATION

Although a Canadian passport is one of the most respected in the world, there are times when a foreign country requires additional documentation (a visa) in order to gain entry into that country.

Check with the appropriate foreign embassy (in Ottawa) or consulate (in most major cities) of the country that you wish to visit in order to verify whether a visa is required. If so, you'll have to visit the embassy or consulate with your passport in order to have the additional documentation provided. Give yourself plenty of time to get this additional paperwork completed. Don't expect a visa to be issued upon demand.

CHAPTER FOUR

At the airport

BEFORE LEAVING

Always check with your airline to determine how soon before your scheduled flight you should be at the airport. The best airplane seats always go to the first travellers in line. Remember, you'll need your ticket and your passport in order to check in.

If you plan to take electronic equipment with you such as cameras, camcorders or portable listening devices, you should register them at the customs desk at the airport before checking in. By registering them, you will have proof that you didn't purchase them on your trip and will thereby avoid unnecessary problems with customs officials both abroad and upon your return. There is also a special counter where you can check in fragile baggage that requires special handling.

Your airline will also be able to tell you about luggage restrictions. If you have excess baggage, you will have to pay by weight.

Many Spanish-speaking countries limit the amount of cigarettes, alcohol, perfume, film and even local currency (foreign currency and traveller's cheques are excluded) that you can bring in. Again, check with your airline or travel agent, or the foreign embassy or consulate, to determine customs regulations in the country to which you are travelling.

Remember that it is a criminal offence to make comments about weapons or hijacking (even in jest); this could cause you serious problems. Save your sparkling wit and **agudezas** (repartee) for your companions on the plane.

UPON ARRIVAL

Customs procedures vary greatly from country to country. Again, your airline or travel agent, or foreign embassies, consulates and tourist offices can give you the information that you seek. **Note:** tourist card applications are often filled out on the plane and simply stamped by customs officials upon your arrival.

The following are some useful phrases that you may use when you arrive at your destination:

Here is my passport.	Aquí tiene mi pasaporte.	ah-**kee tyeh**-neh mee pah-sah-**pohr**-teh
Here is my tourist card.	Aquí tiene mi tarjeta de turista.	ah-**kee tyeh**-neh mee tahr-**heh**-tah deh too-**ree**-stah
I have a visa.	Tengo una visa. (Am)	**tehn**-goh **oo**-nah **bee**-sah (Am)
	Tengo un visado. (Sp)	**tehn**-goh oom bee-**sah**-doh (Sp)
My name is...	Me llamo...	meh **yah**-moh. (Am) meh **lyah**-moh (Sp)
I'm a Canadian.	Soy canadiense.	soy kah-nah-**dyehn**-seh
I'm an American.	Soy norteamericano (a).	soy nohr-teh-ah-meh-ree-**kah**-noh (nah)
I'm on vacation.	Estoy de vacaciones.	eh-**stoy** deh bah-kah-**syoh**-nehs (Am) eh-**stoy** deh bah-kah-**thyoh**-nehs (Sp)
I'm on a business trip.	Estoy en un viaje de negocios.	eh-**stoy** ehn oon **byah**-heh deh neh-**goh**-syohs (Am) eh-**stoy** ehn oon **byah**-heh deh neh-**goh**-thyohs (Sp)

I'm going to be here for...	*Voy a estar aquí por...*	*boy ah eh-**stahr** ah-**kee** pohr*
two days	dos días	dohs **dee**-ahs
one week	una semana	**oo**-nah seh-**mah**-nah
two weeks	dos semanas	dohs seh-**mah**-nahs
one month	un mes	oon mehs
I'm just passing through.	Solamente estoy de paso.	soh-lah-**mehn**-teh eh-**stoy** deh **pah**-soh
I'm going to Peru.	Voy a Perú.	boy ah peh-**roo**
I'm travelling...	*Viajo...*	***byah**-hoh*
alone	solo (a)	**soh**-loh (lah)
with my wife	con mi mujer	kohn mee moo-**hehr**
with my husband	con mi esposo	kohn mee eh-**spoh**-soh
with my children	con mis hijos	kohn mees **ee**-hohs
with my family	con mi familia	kohn mee fah-**mee**-lyah
with my friend	con mi amigo (a)	kohn mee ah-**mee**-goh (gah)
with my friends	con mis amigos (as)	kohn mees ah-**mee**-gohs (gahs)
I'm staying in Barcelona.	Me quedo en Barcelona.	meh **keh**-doh ehn bahr-seh-**loh**-nah (Am) meh **keh**-doh ehn bahr-theh-**loh**-nah (Sp)
I'm staying at the... hotel.	Me quedo en el hotel...	meh **keh**-doh ehn ehl oh-**tehl**
I have nothing to declare.	No tengo nada que declarar.	noh **tehn**-goh **nah**-dah keh deh-klah-**rahr**
I have a bottle of...	Tengo una botella de...	**tehn**-goh **oo**-nah boh-**teh**-yah deh (Am) **tehn**-goh **oo**-nah boh-**teh**-lyah deh (Sp)
I have a carton of cigarettes.	Tengo un cartón de cigarillos.	**tehn**-goh oon kahr-**tohn** deh see-gah-**ree**-yohs (Am) **tehn**-goh oon kahr-**tohn** deh thee-gah-**ree**-lyohs (Sp)

I have some gifts for friends.	Tengo unos regalos para amigos.	**tehn**-goh **oo**-nohs rreh-**gah**-lohs **pah**-rah ah-**mee**-gohs
Here's my baggage claim.	Aquí está mi comprobante.	ah-**kee** eh-**stah** mee kohm-proh-**bahn**-teh
Here's my luggage.	Aquí está mi equipaje.	ah-**kee** eh-**stah** mee eh-kee-**pah**-heh
Here's my suitcase.	Aquí está mi valija. (Am)	ah-**kee** eh-**stah** mee bah-**lee**-hah (Am)
	Aquí está mi maleta. (Sp)	ah-**kee** eh-**stah** mee mah-**leh**-tah (Sp)
Here's my carry-on luggage.	Aquí está mi equipaje de mano.	ah-**kee** eh-**stah** mee eh-kee-**pah**-heh deh **mah**-noh
I'm missing a suitcase.	Me falta una valija. (Am)	meh **fahl**-tah **oo**-nah bah-**lee**-hah (Am)
	Me falta una maleta. (Sp)	meh **fahl**-tah **oo**-nah mah-**leh**-tah (Sp)
I need a luggage cart.	Necesito un carrito para el equipaje.	neh-seh-**see**-toh oon kah-**rree**-toh **pah**-rah ehl eh-kee-**pah**-heh (Am) neh-theh-**see**-toh oon kah-**rree**-toh **pah**-rah ehl eh-kee-**pah**-heh (Sp)
I need a porter.	Necesito un maletero.	neh-seh-**see**-toh oom mah-leh-**teh**-roh (Am) neh-theh-**see**-toh oom mah-leh-**teh**-roh (Sp)
I need a taxi.	Necesito un taxi.	neh-seh-**see**-toh oon **tahk**-see (Am) neh-theh-**see**-toh oon **tahk**-see (Sp)
Where is the taxi stand?	¿Dónde está la parada de taxis?	**dohn**-deh eh-**stah** lah pah-**rah**-dah deh **tahk**-sees

Where is the bus stop?	¿Dónde está la parada de autobús?	**dohn**-deh eh-**stah** lah pah-**rah**-dah deh ow-toh-**boos**
Where is the exit?	¿Dónde está la salida?	**dohn**-deh eh-**stah** lah sah-**lee**-dah

Courtesy and a smile will take you a long way.

Don't forget to say "please."

By tagging on **por favor** (pohr fah-**bohr**) to many of the expressions here, you'll likely get a prompt reply to your request along with a smile in return.

SIGN LANGUAGE

Upon your arrival, you'll see the following signs in airports:

CUSTOMS	ADUANA
IMMIGRATION	INMIGRACIÓN
ESCALATOR	ESCALERA MECÁNICA
UP	ARRIBA
DOWN	ABAJO
ENTRANCE	ENTRADA
EXIT	SALIDA
MEN'S ROOM	CABALLEROS
LADIES' ROOM	DAMAS/SEÑORAS
PUSH	EMPUJE
PULL	TIRE
	JALE (México)
CAR RENTALS	ALQUILER DE AUTOS
DUTY FREE SHOP	TIENDA LIBRE DE IMPUESTOS

CHAPTER FIVE

At the hotel

Hotels in Spain, Mexico and parts of Latin America are rated on a five-star system, five stars indicating a deluxe location and one star indicating a very modest one. Travellers to Spain can obtain a list of hotels and their ratings through the Spanish National Tourist Office (located in many large cities). Travel agents, national tourist offices, embassies and consulates may also prove helpful when seeking hotel accommodation in Latin American destinations.

For tourists with an unlimited budget, Spain offers **paradores**, luxury hotels located in converted castles or monasteries. Mexico has similar spots, **posadas**, located in former monasteries or haciendas. All of these accommodations are extremely well equipped and have every modern convenience. Throughout the Spanish-speaking world, large, American-style highrise hotels also exist. These hotels offer every amenity to their guests (gift shops, coffee shops, fine dining rooms, exercise rooms and some even have pools).

You'll find that many hotels will claim that the water in the taps is purified and safe for drinking. However, to avoid any risks, bottled water in a sealed container is still your best bet.

Travellers on a more limited budget have a variety of accommodations from which to choose. Here is a list of the different accommodation types:

a luxury government-run hotel	parador (Spain)	pah-rah-**dohr**
a luxury hotel	posada (Mexico)	poh-**sah**-dah
a standard hotel	hotel	oh-**tehl**
a small modestly-priced hotel	albergue	ahl-**behr**-geh
a guesthouse (meals included)	pensión	pehn-**syohn**

rural, rustic accommodation	refugio	rreh-**foo**-hyoh
a youth hostel (low prices)	albergue juvenil	ahl-**behr**-geh hoo-beh-**neel**
a youth hostel	hostal	oh-**stahl**
student residence	residencia estudiantil	rreh-see-**dehn**-syah eh-stoo-dyahn-**teel** (Am) rreh-see-**dehn**-thyah eh-stoo-dyahn-**teel** (Sp)

Most universities in the Spanish-speaking world do not have student residences. However, some do exist and offer very reasonable rates for travelling students. In addition, if you're planning to stay in youth hostels or other inexpensive accommodations, keep in mind that towels, soap and shampoo are often not supplied. You'd be wise to pack these items in your luggage before you leave on your trip.

Don't forget to use the greetings and expressions of courtesy (see "The Basics"). **Buenos días, por favor, muchas gracias** and a smile work wonders in Spanish-speaking countries.

I have a reservation.	Tengo una reservación. (Am)	**tehn**-goh **oo**-nah rreh-sehr-bah-**syohn** (Am)
	Tengo una reserva. (Sp)	**tehn**-goh **oo**-nah rreh-**sehr**-bah (Sp)
I don't have a reservation.	No tengo reservación. (Am)	noh **tehn**-goh rreh-sehr-bah-**syohn** (Am)
	No tengo reserva. (Sp)	noh **tehn**-goh rreh-**sehr**-bah (Sp)
I'd like a room...	*Quisiera una habitación...*	*kee-**syeh**-rah **oo**-nah ah-bee-tah-**syohn** (Am)*
		*kee-**syeh**-rah **oo**-nah ah-bee-tah-**thyohn** (Sp)*
with one bed	con una sola cama	kohn **oo**-nah **soh**-lah **kah**-mah

I'd like a room...	*Quisiera una habitación...*	*kee-**syeh**-rah **oo**-nah ah-bee-tah-**syohn** (Am)* *kee-**syeh**-rah **oo**-nah ah-bee-tah-**thyohn** (Sp)*
with two beds	doble	**doh**-bleh
with air-conditioning	con aire acondicionado	kohn **ahy**-reh ah-kohn-dee-syoh-**nah**-doh (Am) kohn **ahy**-reh ah-kohn-dee-thyoh-**nah**-doh (Sp)
with heat	con calefacción	kohn kah-leh-fahk -**syohn** (Am) kohn kah-leh-fahk-**thyohn** (Sp)
with a shower	con ducha	kohn **doo**-chah
with a private bath	con baño privado	kohn **bah**-nyoh pree-**bah**-doh
with hot water	con agua caliente	kohn **ah**-gwah kah-**lyehn**-teh
with TV	con televisión	kohn teh-leh-bee-**syohn**
that is quiet	tranquila	trahn-**kee**-lah
facing the street	con vista a la calle	kohn **bee**-stah ah lah **kah**-yeh (Am) kohn **bee**-stah ah lah **kah**-lyeh (Sp)
facing the ocean	con vista al mar	kohn **bee**-stah ahl mahr
facing the patio	con vista al patio	kohn **bee**-stah ahl **pah**-tyoh
for tonight	por esta noche	pohr **eh**-stah **noh**-cheh
for one night	por una noche	pohr **oo**-nah **noh**-cheh
for two nights	por dos noches	pohr dohs **noh**-chehs
for one week	por una semana	pohr **oo**-nah seh-**mah**-nah
for two weeks	por dos semanas	pohr dohs seh-**mah**-nahs

Water faucets are marked C and F in Spanish-speaking countries. Automatically, the weary traveller turns to the C tap for cold water. In fact, C stands for **caliente** or "hot," F for **frío** or "cold."

How much is it...?	*¿Cuánto cuesta...?*	***kwahn**-toh **kweh**-stah*
per night	por noche	pohr **noh**-cheh
per week	por semana	pohr seh-**mah**-nah
May I see the room?	¿Puedo ver la habitación?	**pweh**-doh behr lah ah-bee-tah-**syohn** (Am) **pweh**-doh behr lah ah-bee-tah-**thyohn** (Sp)
What floor is it on?	¿En qué piso está?	ehn keh **pee**-soh eh-**stah**
Is there an elevator?	¿Hay un ascensor?	ahy oon ah-sehn-**sohr** (Am) ahy oon ahs-thehn-**sohr** (Sp)
I'd like another room.	Quiero cambiar de habitación.	**kyeh**-roh kahm-**byahr** deh ah-bee-tah-**syohn** (Am) **kyeh**-roh kahm-**byahr** deh ah-bee-tah-**thyohn** (Sp)
Do you have something...?	*¿Hay algo...?*	*ahy **ahl**-goh*
bigger	más grande	mahs **grahn**-deh
smaller	más pequeño	mahs peh-**keh**-nyoh
less expensive	más barato	mahs bah-**rah**-toh
more expensive	más caro	mahs **kah**-roh
quieter	más tranquilo	mahs trahn-**kee**-loh
What's my room number, please?	¿Cuál es el número de mi habitación, por favor?	kwahl ehs ehl **noo**-meh-roh deh mee ah-bee-tah-**syohn** pohr fah-**bohr** (Am) kwahl ehs ehl **noo**-meh-roh deh mee ah-bee-tah-**thyohn** pohr fah-**bohr** (Sp)
May I have my key?	Mi llave, por favor.	mee **yah**-beh pohr fah-**bohr** (Am) mee **lyah**-beh pohr fah-**bohr** (Sp)
I've lost my key.	He perdido mi llave.	eh pehr-**dee**-doh mee **yah**-beh (Am) eh pehr-**dee**-doh mee **lyah**-beh (Sp)

I need a bellhop.	Necesito un botones.	neh-seh-**see**-toh oom boh-**toh**-nehs (Am) neh-theh-**see**-toh oom boh-**toh**-nehs (Sp)
I need a chambermaid.	Necesito una camarera.	neh-seh-**see**-toh **oo**-nah kah-mah-**reh**-rah (Am) neh-theh-**see**-toh **oo**-nah kah-mah-**reh**-rah
Is the service included?	¿Está incluido el servicio?	eh-**stah** een-**klwee**-doh ehl sehr-**bee**-syoh (Am) eh-**stah** een-**klwee**-doh ehl sehr-**bee**-thyoh (Sp)
Is breakfast included?	¿Está incluido el desayuno?	eh-**stah** een-**klwee**-doh ehl deh-sah-**yoo**-noh
Is lunch included?	¿Está incluido el almuerzo?	eh-**stah** een-**klwee**-doh ehl ahl-**mwehr**-soh (Am) eh-**stah** een-**klwee**-doh ehl ahl-**mwehr**-thoh (Sp)
Is dinner included?	¿Está incluido la cena?	eh-**stah** een-**klwee**-doh lah **seh**-nah (Am) eh-**stah** een-**klwee**-doh lah **theh**-nah (Sp)
What time do you serve...?	*¿A qué hora sirven...?*	*ah keh **oh**-rah **seer**-behn*
breakfast	el desayuno	ehl deh-sah-**yoo**-noh
lunch	el almuerzo	ehl ahl-**mwehr**-soh (Am) ehl ahl-**mwehr**-thoh (Sp)
dinner	la cena	lah **seh**-nah (Am) lah **theh**-nah (Sp)
Do you have room service?	¿Hay servicio de habitación?	ahy sehr-**bee**-syoh deh ah-bee-tah-**syohn** (Am) ahy sehr-**bee**-thyoh deh ah-bee-tah-**thyohn** (Sp)
Do you have a safety deposit box?	¿Hay una caja de valores?	ahy **oo**-nah **kah**-hah deh bah-**loh**-rehs
I'd like to leave this in your safety deposit box.	Quisiera dejar esto en su caja de valores.	kee-**syeh**-rah deh-**hahr** **eh**-stoh ehn soo **kah**-hah deh bah-**loh**-rehs

Do you have laundry service?	¿Hay servicio de lavandería?	ahy sehr-**bee**-syoh deh lah-bahn-deh-**ree**-ah (Am) ahy sehr-**bee**-thyoh deh lah-bahn-deh-**ree**-ah (Sp)
Could you wake me at seven o'clock, please?	¿Podría despertarme a las siete, por favor?	poh-**dree**-ah deh-spehr-**tahr**-meh ah lahs **syeh**-teh pohr fah-**bohr**
I need...	*Necesito...*	*neh-seh-**see**-toh (Am)* *neh-theh-**see**-toh (Sp)*
an extra bed	otra cama	**oh**-trah **kah**-mah
an ashtray	un cenicero	oon seh-nee-**seh**-roh (Am) oon theh-nee-**theh**-roh (Sp)
a bar of soap	una pastilla de jabón	**oo**-nah pah-**stee**-yah deh hah-**bohn** (Am) **oo**-nah pah-**stee**-lyah deh hah-**bohn** (Sp)
a blanket	una manta	**oo**-nah **mahn**-tah
some hangers	unas perchas	**oo**-nahs **pehr**-chahs
a pillow	una almohada	**oo**-nah ahl-moh-**ah**-dah
toilet paper	papel higiénico	pah-**pehl** ee-**hyeh**-nee-koh
a towel	una toalla	**oo**-nah toh-**ah**-yah (Am) **oo**-nah toh-**ah**-lyah (Sp)
Where's the nearest...?	*¿Dónde está...?*	***dohn**-deh eh-**stah***
laundromat	la lavandería más cercana	lah lah-bahn-deh-**ree**-ah mahs sehr-**kah**-nah (Am) lah lah-bahn-deh-**ree**-ah más thehr-**kah**-nah (Sp)
public telephone	el teléfono público más cercano	ehl teh-**leh**-foh-noh **poo**-blee-koh mahs sehr-**kah**-noh (Am) ehl teh-**leh**-foh-noh **poo**-blee-koh mahs thehr-**kah**-noh (Sp)
pharmacy	la farmacia más cercana	lah fahr-**mah**-syah mahs sehr-**kah**-nah (Am) lah fahr-**mah**-thyah mahs thehr-**kah**-nah (Sp)

Where's the nearest...?	*¿Dónde está...?*	***dohn**-deh eh-**stah***
good restaurant	un buen restaurante que está cerca	oon bwehn rreh-stow-**rahn**-teh keh eh-**stah sehr**-kah (Am) oon bwehn rreh-stow-**rahn**-teh keh eh-**stah thehr**-kah (Sp)
money exchange	el cambio más cercano	ehl **kahm**-byoh mahs sehr-**kah**-noh (Am) ehl **kahm**-byoh mahs thehr-**kah**-noh (Sp)
I'm checking out tomorrow morning at nine o'clock.	Salgo mañana por la mañana a las nueve.	**sahl**-goh mah-**nyah**-nah pohr lah mah-**nyah**-nah ah lahs **nweh**-beh
I'd like to pay my bill.	Quisiera pagar mi cuenta.	kee-**syeh**-rah pah-**gahr** mee **kwehn**-tah
Can you order me a taxi, please?	¿Puede llamarme un taxi, por favor?	**pweh**-deh yah-**mahr**-meh oon **tahk**-see pohr fah-**bohr** (Am) **pweh**-deh lyah-**mahr**-meh oon **tahk**-see pohr fah-**bohr** (Sp)

SIGN LANGUAGE

You'll see the following signs in many hotels:

FRONT DESK	RECEPCIÓN
CASHIER	CAJA
ELEVATOR	ASCENSOR
MEN'S ROOM	CABALLEROS
LADIES' ROOM	DAMAS/SEÑORAS
WASHROOMS	SERVICIOS
DINING ROOM	COMEDOR

It is customary to tip the bellhop and the chambermaid in most hotels. However, tipping procedures vary from country to country. Check with your travel agent to determine the going rate for the services that these people provide.

CHAPTER SIX

Travelling

Public transportation in most cities offers you an inexpensive way to do your sightseeing. Madrid, Barcelona, Mexico City, Caracas and Buenos Aires all have metro (subway) systems that are reasonably priced and efficient. Mexico City's metro is very modern. Trains run on rubber wheels and the stations are decorated with art. One station south of the Zócalo boasts an Aztec temple that was discovered during excavations for the station's construction.

Maps of bus and metro routes are available in most hotels, at newsstand kiosks, as well as at many metro stops. The metro systems are well planned and the maps are very easy to follow. Bus routes may be a bit more confusing to travellers, especially if you don't have a great sense of direction, but the desk clerk in your hotel can tell you which bus routes to take. Very often, hotel personnel will prove to be an important source of information in your travels. Don't hesitate to ask for information or recommendations - often they can reply in English, Spanish and many other languages.

Taxis are more direct than buses and metros, but will cost two or three times more than public transit. For personal safety, it may be a good idea to use a taxi to return to your hotel late at night, especially if it's located off the beaten track. Some taxis have meters and charge accordingly; others charge by zone. Many taxis charge extra for luggage. If your taxi is not equipped with a meter, you should negotiate the cost of your trip before you start off. You'll find this phrase very useful when negotiating the price:

How much is it to go to...?	¿Cuánto es para ir a...?	**kwahn**-toh ehs **pah**-rah eer ah

TAKING THE BUS

Don't forget to use the greetings and expressions of courtesy (see "The Basics"). **Por favor, gracias** and a smile are great icebreakers in Spanish-speaking countries.

Where's the bus stop?	¿Dónde está la parada de autobús?	**dohn**-deh eh-**stah** lah pah-**rah**-dah deh ow-toh-**boos**
Where's the bus station?	¿Dónde está la estación de autobuses?	**dohn**-deh eh-**stah** lah eh-stah-**syohn** deh ow-toh-**boo**-sehs (Am) **dohn**-deh eh-**stah** lah eh-stah-**thyohn** deh ow-toh-**boo**-sehs (Sp)
	¿Dónde está la camionera?	**dohn**-deh eh-**stah** la kah-myoh-**neh**-rah (Mexico)
Where can I buy bus tickets?	¿Dónde puedo comprar boletos de autobús? (Am)	**dohn**-deh **pweh**-doh kohm-**prahr** boh-**leh**-tohs deh ow-toh-**boos** (Am)
	¿Dónde puedo comprar billetes de autobús? (Sp)	**dohn**-deh **pweh**-doh kohm-**prahr** bee-**lyeh**-tehs deh ow-toh-**boos** (Sp)
How much does a ticket cost?	¿Cuánto cuesta un boleto? (Am)	**kwahn**-toh **kweh**-stah oon boh-**leh**-toh (Am)
	¿Cuánto cuesta un billete? (Sp)	**kwahn**-toh **kweh**-stah oon bee-**lyeh**-teh(Sp)
Do I need the exact change?	¿Necesito cambio exacto?	neh-seh-**see**-toh **kahm**-byoh ehk-**sahk**-toh (Am) neh-theh-**see**-toh **kahm**-byoh ehk-**sahk**-toh (Sp)
I want to go to...	Quiero ir a...	**kyeh**-roh eer ah
Which bus do I take?	¿Qué autobús debo tomar?	keh ow-toh-**boos** **deh**-boh toh-**mahr**

Where do I get off?	¿Dónde debo bajarme?	**dohn**-deh **deh**-boh bah-**hahr**-meh
Can you please tell me when to get off?	¿Puede decirme cuándo debo bajarme?	**pweh**-deh deh-**seer**-meh **kwahn**-doh **deh**-boh bah-**hahr**-meh (Am) **pweh**-deh deh-**theer**-meh **kwahn**-doh **deh**-boh bah-**hahr**-meh (Sp)
Do I have to transfer?	¿Tengo que cambiar?	**tehn**-goh keh kahm-**byahr**
How often do the buses run?	¿Con qué frecuencia salen los autobuses?	kohn keh freh-**kwehn**-syah **sah**-lehn lohs ow-toh-**boo**-sehs (Am) kohn keh freh-**kwehn**-thyah **sah**-lehn lohs ow-toh-**boo**-sehs (Sp)

The word for a local city bus varies greatly from country to country. The expressions in this section use the word **autobús,** but you will also hear the following words in your travels.

autobús	ow-toh-**boos**	Colombia, Spain, Venezuela
camión	kah-**myohn**	Mexico
camioneta	kah-myoh-**neh**-tah	Guatemala
casadoro	kah-sah-**doh**-roh	Costa Rica
colectivo	koh-lehk-**tee**-boh	Argentina, Bolivia
góndola	**gohn**-doh-lah	Chile
guagua	**gwah**-gwah	Canary Islands, Cuba
micro	**mee**-kroh	Chile
ómnibus	**ohm**-nee-boos	Peru
omnibús	ohm-nee-**boos**	Uruguay

TAKING THE METRO (SUBWAY)

The metro is an inexpensive and efficient way to get around most major cities. The stations are clean and comfortable. The various routes are clearly marked so that it's fairly easy to figure out which line to take. Remember that Mexico City has a population in excess of 25 million inhabitants, so morning and evening rush hours are good times to avoid when travelling on this system.

Is there a metro station nearby?	¿Hay una estación de metro cerca?	ahy **oo**-nah eh-stah-**syohn** deh **meh**-troh **sehr**-kah (Am) ahy **oo**-nah eh-stah-**thyohn** deh **meh**-troh **thehr**-kah (Sp)
Where's the nearest metro station?	¿Dónde está la estación de metro más cercana?	**dohn**-deh eh-**stah** lah eh-stah-**syohn** deh **meh**-troh mahs sehr-**kah**-nah (Am) **dohn**-deh eh-**stah** lah eh-stah-**thyohn** deh **meh**-troh mahs thehr-**kah**-nah (Sp)
Where can I buy metro tokens?	¿Dónde puedo comprar fichas de metro?	**dohn**-deh **pweh**-doh kohm-**prahr** **fee**-chahs deh **meh**-troh
How much are they?	¿Cuánto cuestan?	**kwahn**-toh **kweh**-stahn
Which line should I take to go to...	¿Qué línea debo tomar para ir a...	keh **lee**-neh-ah **deh**-boh toh-**mahr** **pah**-rah eer ah
Do I have to change lines?	¿Debo cambiar de línea?	**deh**-boh kahm-**byahr** deh **lee**-neh-ah

What's the next station?	¿Cuál es la próxima estación?	kwahl ehs lah **prohk**-see-mah eh-stah-**syohn** (Am) kwahl ehs lah **prohk**-see-mah eh-stah-**thyohn** (Sp)
What's the final station?	¿Cuál es la última estación?	kwahl ehs lah **ool**-tee-mah eh-stah-**syohn** (Am) kwahl ehs lah **ool**-tee-mah eh-stah-**thyohn** (Sp)
What time does the metro open?	¿A qué hora se abre el metro?	ah keh **oh**-rah seh **ah**-breh ehl **meh**-troh
What time does the metro close?	¿A qué hora se cierra el metro?	ah keh **oh**-rah seh **syeh**-rrah ehl **meh**-troh (Am) ah keh **oh**-rah seh **thyeh**-rrah ehl **meh**-troh (Sp)
What time does the last train leave?	¿A qué hora sale el último tren?	ah keh **oh**-rah **sah**-leh ehl **ool**-tee-moh trehn
Where's the exit?	¿Dónde está la salida?	**dohn**-deh eh-**stah** lah sah-**lee**-dah

TAKING A TAXI

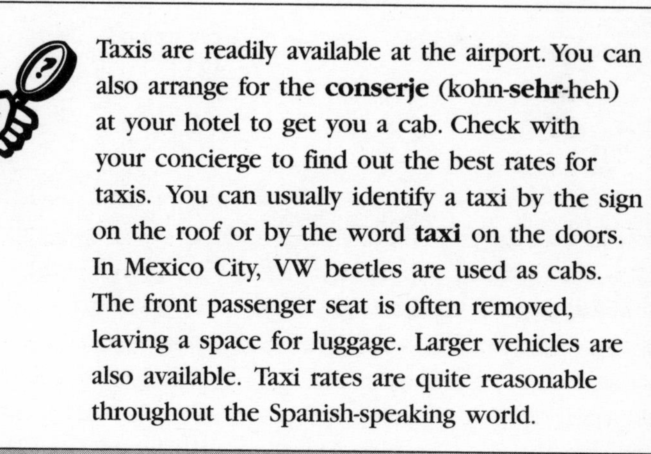

Taxis are readily available at the airport. You can also arrange for the **conserje** (kohn-**sehr**-heh) at your hotel to get you a cab. Check with your concierge to find out the best rates for taxis. You can usually identify a taxi by the sign on the roof or by the word **taxi** on the doors. In Mexico City, VW beetles are used as cabs. The front passenger seat is often removed, leaving a space for luggage. Larger vehicles are also available. Taxi rates are quite reasonable throughout the Spanish-speaking world.

TAKING A TAXI

English	Spanish	Pronunciation
Where's a taxi stand?	¿Dónde hay una parada de taxis?	**dohn**-deh ahy **oo**-nah pah-**rah**-dah deh **tahk**-sees
I need a taxi.	Necesito un taxi.	neh-seh-**see**-toh oon **tahk**-see (Am) neh-theh-**see**-toh oon **tahk**-see (Sp)
Can you please call me a taxi?	¿Puede llamarme un taxi, por favor?	**pweh**-deh yah-**mahr**-meh oon **tahk**-see pohr fah-**bohr** (Am) **pweh**-deh lyah-**mahr**-meh oon **tahk**-see pohr fah-**bohr** (Sp)
Is the taxi available?	¿Está libre?	eh-**stah lee**-breh
I want to go...	*Quiero ir...*	***kyeh**-roh eer*
downtown	al centro	ahl **sehn**-troh (Am) ahl **thehn**-troh (Sp)
to the airport	al aeropuerto	ahl ah-eh-roh-**pwehr**-toh
to the hotel	al hotel	ahl oh-**tehl**
to the bus station	a la estación de autobuses	ah lah eh-stah-**syohn** deh ow-toh-**boo**-sehs (Am) ah lah eh-stah-**thyohn** deh ow-toh-**boo**-sehs (Sp)
to the train station	a la estación de trenes	ah lah eh-stah-**syohn** deh **treh**-nehs (Am) ah lah eh-stah-**thyohn** deh **treh**-nehs (Sp)
to... Street	a la calle...	ah lah **kah**-yeh (Am) ah lah **kah**-lyeh (Sp)
to 5th Avenue.	a la Quinta Avenida.	ah lah **keen**-tah ah-beh-**nee**-dah
How much is it to go...?	*¿Cuánto es para ir...?*	***kwahn**-toh ehs **pah**-rah eer*
to the airport	al aeropuerto	ahl ah-eh-roh-**pwehr**-toh
to the museum	al museo	ahl moo-**seh**-oh
downtown	al centro	ahl **sehn**-troh (Am) ahl **thehn**-troh (Sp)

Slower, please.	Más despacio, por favor.	mahs deh-**spah**-syoh pohr fah-**bohr** (Am) mahs deh-**spah**-thyoh pohr fah-**bohr** (Sp)
Faster, please.	Más rápido, por favor.	mahs **rrah**-pee-doh pohr fah-**bohr**
Stop here, please.	Pare aquí, por favor.	**pah**-reh ah-**kee** pohr fah-**bohr**
Stop over there, please.	Pare allá, por favor.	**pah**-reh ah-**yah** pohr fah-**bohr** (Am) **pah**-reh ah-**lyah** pohr fah-**bohr** (Sp)
Stop at the corner.	Pare en la esquina.	**pah**-reh ehn lah eh-**skee**-nah
How much is it?	¿Cuánto es?	**kwahn**-toh ehs
This is for you.	Esto es para usted.	**eh**-stoh ehs **pah**-rah oo-**stehd**

It is customary to tip the cab driver. In Mexico and Latin America, a small tip is in order. In Spain, you should give the driver a 10 percent tip. Metered taxi fares must be paid as they roll up; unmetered fares are by zone or negotiated.

TAKING A FLIGHT

The following are some useful phrases that you may use when you plan further air travel from a Spanish-speaking country:

I'd like to buy a ticket for...	Me gustaría comprar un boleto para...(Am)	meh goo-stah-**ree**-ah kohm-**prahr** oom boh-**leh**-toh **pah**-rah (Am)
	Me gustaría comprar un billete para...(Sp)	meh goo-stah-**ree**-ah kohm-**prahr** oom bee-**lyeh**-teh **pah**-rah (Sp)
I'd like a one-way ticket.	Quisiera un boleto de ida. (Am)	kee-**syeh**-rah oom boh-**leh**-toh deh **ee**-dah (Am)
	Quisiera un billete de ida. (Sp)	kee-**syeh**-rah oom bee-**lyeh**-teh deh **ee**-dah (Sp)

I'd like a round trip ticket.	Quisiera un boleto de ida y vuelta. (Am)	kee-**syeh**-rah oom boh-**leh**-toh deh **ee**-dah ee **bwehl**-tah (Am)
	Quisiera un billete de ida y vuelta. (Sp)	kee-**syeh**-rah oom bee-**lyeh**-teh deh **ee**-dah ee **bwehl**-tah (Sp)
I'd like a first-class ticket.	Quisiera un boleto de primera clase. (Am)	kee-**syeh**-rah oom boh-**leh**-toh deh pree-**meh**-rah **klah**-seh (Am)
	Quisiera un billete de primera clase. (Sp)	kee-**syeh**-rah oom bee-**lyeh**-teh deh pree-**meh**-rah **klah**-seh (Sp)
I'd like a tourist-class ticket.	Quisiera un boleto de clase turística. (Am)	kee-**syeh**-rah oom boh-**leh**-toh deh **klah**-seh too-**ree**-stee-kah (Am)
	Quisiera un billete de clase turística. (Sp)	kee-**syeh**-rah oom bee-**lyeh**-teh deh **klah**-seh too-**ree**-stee-kah (Sp)
I want an aisle seat.	Quiero un asiento al pasillo.	**kyeh**-roh oon ah-**syehn**-toh ahl pah-**see**-yoh (Am)
		kyeh-roh oon ah-**syehn**-toh ahl pah-**see**-lyoh (Sp)
I want a window seat.	Quiero un asiento a la ventanilla.	**kyeh**-roh oon ah-**syehn**-toh ah lah behn-tah-**nee**-yah (Am)
		kyeh-roh oon ah-**syehn**-toh ah lah behn-tah-**nee**-lyah (Sp)

I'd like a seat in the smoking section.	Quisiera un asiento en la sección de fumar.	kee-**syeh**-rah oon ah-**syehn**-toh ehn lah sehk-**syohn** deh foo-**mahr** (Am) kee-**syeh**-rah oon ah-**syehn**-toh ehn lah sehk-**thyohn** deh foo-**mahr** (Sp)
I'd like a seat in the non-smoking section.	Quisiera un asiento en la sección de no fumar.	kee-**syeh**-rah oon ah-**syehn**-toh ehn lah sehk-**syohn** deh noh foo-**mahr** (Am) kee-**syeh**-rah oon ah-**syehn**-toh ehn lah sehk-**thyohn** deh noh foo-**mahr** (Sp)
Is it a direct flight?	¿Es un vuelo directo?	ehs oon **bweh**-loh dee-**rehk**-toh
Does it make stops?	¿Hace escalas?	**ah**-seh eh-**skah**-lahs (Am) **ah**-theh eh-**skah**-lahs (Sp)

SIGN LANGUAGE

You'll see the following signs in airports:

ARRIVALS	LLEGADAS
DEPARTURES	SALIDAS
INTERNATIONAL FLIGHTS	VUELOS INTERNACIONALES
NATIONAL FLIGHTS	VUELOS NACIONALES
DEPARTURE GATE	PUERTA DE SALIDA
CUSTOMS	ADUANA
DUTY FREE SHOP	TIENDA LIBRE DE IMPUESTOS

TRAINS AND BUSES

Spain is an extremely mountainous country, second only to Switzerland in all of Europe. Train travel in Spain is both efficient and convenient and offers the tourist magnificent scenery and breathtaking vistas. The RENFE (**Red Nacional de Ferrocarriles Españoles** - Spanish national railroad network) offers discount fares that are related to the distance travelled. Eurailpasses are accepted in Spain as well as other European countries and offer unlimited train travel of varying duration. If you are contemplating a Eurailpass, you should make arrangements with your travel agent before leaving. If you've purchased a Eurailpass, don't assume that you'll automatically have a seat on the train. Reservations are often required. You won't want to stand on the train while travelling from Barcelona to Lisbon. If you know your schedule in advance, you can make Eurailpass reservations before you even leave the country.

Spain offers a variety of train services appealing to a wide range of budgets. The following are some of the services provided:

Talgo	an air-conditioned luxury express operating between Madrid and most major cities
Electrotrén	an air-conditioned luxury train that is slower and less expensive than the Talgo, making more stops and covering a greater area
TER	another luxury express that is slower and makes more stops than the Talgo
TAF	a second-class diesel train
Expreso	a long-distance night train that makes a few stops
Rápido	a fast train (slower and makes more stops than the Expreso)
Ferrobuses	local trains

Train travel in Mexico is not as reliable as the Spanish rail services. Government cutbacks and privatization of rail services have forced the cancellation of many routes. Those that remain do not always adhere to their scheduled departure and arrival times. An Internet search for Mexican National Railways should give you up-to-date information on train travel in Mexico. You may have heard the Mexican song *La cucaracha* which dates back to the Mexican Revolution of 1910. The song pokes fun at the Revolutionary armies of Pancho Villa and of Venustiano Carranza, and in particular, of Pancho Villa's old train which was nicknamed "La cucharacha." In the song, the train could no longer run because it lacked the necessary power to do so. A century later, things haven't changed that much. However, Mexico does offer a first-rate bus system between major centres as well as a variety of air flights that more than adequately meet the needs of travellers.

In other parts of Latin America, bus travel seems to be far more common than rail travel. Modern highway coaches travel between major centres but, at times, the buses will be crowded and almost broken down, especially in rural areas. They will get you where you want to go, but with varying degrees of comfort.

Where's the train station?	¿Dónde está la estación de ferrocarril?	**dohn**-deh eh-**stah** lah eh-stah-**syohn** deh feh-rroh-kah-**rreel** (Am) **dohn**-deh eh-**stah** lah eh-stah-**thyohn** deh feh-rroh-kah-**rreel** (Sp)
Where's the ticket window?	¿Dónde está la boletería? (Am)	**dohn**-deh eh-**stah** lah boh-leh-teh-**ree**-ah (Am)
	¿Dónde está la ventanilla? (Sp)	**dohn**-deh eh-**stah** lah behn-tah-**nee**-lyah (Sp)
I'd like to buy a ticket for...	Me gustaría comprar un boleto para...(Am)	meh goo-stah-**ree**-ah kohm-**prahr** oom boh-**leh**-toh **pah**-rah (Am)
	Me gustaría comprar un billete para...(Sp)	meh goo-stah-**ree**-ah kohm-**prahr** oom bee-**lyeh**-teh **pah**-rah (Sp)
I'd like a one-way ticket.	Quisiera un boleto de ida. (Am)	kee-**syeh**-rah oom boh-**leh**-toh deh **ee**-dah (Am)
	Quisiera un billete de ida. (Sp)	kee-**syeh**-rah oom bee-**lyeh**-teh deh **ee**-dah (Sp)
I'd like a round trip ticket.	Quisiera un boleto de ida y vuelta. (Am)	kee-**syeh**-rah oom boh-**leh**-toh deh **ee**-dah ee **bwehl**-tah (Am)

I'd like a round trip ticket.	Quisiera un billete de ida y vuelta. (Sp)	kee-**syeh**-rah oom bee-**lyeh**-teh deh **ee**-dah ee **bwehl**-tah (Sp)
I'd like a first-class ticket.	Quisiera un boleto de primera clase. (Am)	kee-**syeh**-rah oom boh-**leh**-toh deh pree-**meh**-rah **klah**-seh (Am)
	Quisiera un billete de primera clase. (Sp)	kee-**syeh**-rah oom bee-**lyeh**-teh deh pree-**meh**-rah **klah**-seh (Sp)
I'd like a second-class ticket.	Quisiera un boleto de segunda clase. (Am)	kee-**syeh**-rah oom boh-**leh**-toh deh seh-**goon**-dah **klah**-seh (Am)
	Quisiera un billete de segunda clase. (Sp)	kee-**syeh**-rah oom bee-**lyeh**-teh deh seh-**goon**-dah **klah**-seh (Sp)
Is it an express train?	¿Es un tren expreso?	ehs oon trehn ehk-**spreh**-soh (Am) ehs oon trehn eh-**spreh**-soh (Sp)
Is it a local train?	¿Es un tren local?	ehs oon trehn loh-**kahl**
Is it a through train?	¿Es un tren directo?	ehs oon trehn dee-**rehk**-toh
Do I have to transfer?	¿Tengo que hacer transbordo?	**tehn**-goh keh ah-**sehr** trahns-**bohr**-doh (Am) **tehn**-goh keh ah-**thehr** trahns-**bohr**-doh (Sp)
Does the train stop in...?	¿Para el tren en...?	**pah**-rah ehl trehn ehn
Is there a non-smoking compartment?	¿Hay un compartimiento de no fumar? (Am)	ahy oon kohm-pahr-tee-**myehn**-toh deh noh foo-**mahr** (Am)
	¿Hay un compartimento de no fumar? (Sp)	ahy oon kohm-pahr-tee-**mehn**-toh deh noh foo-**mahr** (Sp)

What time does the train leave for...?	¿A qué hora sale el tren para...?	ah keh **oh**-rah **sah**-leh ehl trehn **pah**-rah
What time does the train from...arrive?	¿A qué hora llega el tren de...?	ah keh **oh**-rah **yeh**-gah ehl trehn deh (Am) ah keh **oh**-rah **lyeh**-gah ehl trehn deh (Sp)
What platform does the train leave from?	¿De qué andén sale el tren?	deh keh ahn-**dehn** **sah**-leh ehl trehn
What platform does the train arrive at?	¿A qué andén llega el tren?	ah keh ahn-**dehn** **yeh**-gah ehl trehn (Am) ah keh ahn-**dehn** **lyeh**-gah ehl trehn (Sp)
Is this seat taken?	¿Está ocupado este asiento?	eh-**stah** oh-koo-**pah**-doh **eh**-steh ah-**syehn**-toh (Am) eh-**stah** oh-koo-**pah**-doh **eh**-steh ah-**thyehn**-toh (Sp)
Where is the dining car?	¿Dónde está el coche restaurante? (Am)	**dohn**-deh eh-**stah** ehl **koh**-cheh rreh-stow-**rahn**-teh (Am)
	¿Dónde está el coche-comedor? (Sp)	**dohn**-deh eh-**stah** ehl **koh**-cheh koh-meh-**dohr** (Sp)
Where is the sleeping car?	¿Dónde está el coche-dormitorio? (Am)	**dohn**-deh eh-**stah** ehl **koh**-cheh dohr-mee-**toh**-ryoh (Am)
	¿Dónde está el coche-cama?(Sp)	**dohn**-deh eh-**stah** ehl **koh**-cheh **kah**-mah (Sp)
Are we going to arrive...?	*¿Vamos a llegar...?*	***bah**-mohs ah yeh-**gahr** (Am) **bah**-mohs ah lyeh-**gahr** (Sp)*
early	temprano	tehm-**prah**-noh
on time	a tiempo	ah **tyehm**-poh
late	tarde	**tahr**-deh

SIGN LANGUAGE

You'll see the following signs in train stations:

TICKET COUNTER	BOLETERÍA (Am)
	TAQUILLA (Sp)
	VENTANILLA
SCHEDULE	HORARIO
ARRIVALS	LLEGADAS
DEPARTURES	SALIDAS
PLATFORM	ANDÉN
TRACK	VÍA
EMERGENCY EXIT	SALIDA DE EMERGENCIA
NO SMOKING	PROHIBIDO FUMAR

TRAVELLING BY CAR

Car rentals

If you're planning to rent a car on your trip, you can save money by making arrangements before you leave. Your travel agent will help you get the best deals available in car rentals. Car rental agencies are also available in most major airports so, if you make a last-minute decision to rent, you can do so upon your arrival. A valid driver's licence and credit card are usually all that is needed. However, it would be a good idea to verify if an international driver's licence is required should you plan to travel extensively with rental cars. Some age restrictions may also be a factor in renting a car; so don't assume that just because you have a driver's licence, you can automatically rent a car.

Insurance is an absolute must. Automobile liability insurance is mandatory and proof of coverage should be kept on your person while driving. Become familiar with the vehicle that you are renting as well as with road signs and the rules of the road before you start off. As a foreign traveller, you should always obey the law, even if the local population does not.

Many Spanish-speaking countries have road signs that conform with the international system. Argentina, Cuba, the Dominican Republic, Ecuador, Morocco and Spain presently use the international system. Chile is adapting to this system as well. In the future, you'll find more and more countries using this system. You can get a copy of these international road signs at any automobile association office (CAA or AAA).

Where can I rent a car?	¿Dónde puedo alquilar un auto?	**dohn**-deh **pweh**-doh ahl-kee-**lahr** oon **ow**-toh
I'd like to rent a car.	Quisiera alquilar un carro. (Am)	kee-**syeh**-rah ahl-kee-**lahr** oon **kah**-rroh (Am)
	Quisiera alquilar un coche. (Sp)	kee-**syeh**-rah ahl-kee-**lahr** oon **koh**-cheh (Sp)
I'd like a compact car.	Quisiera un auto pequeño.	kee-**syeh**-rah oon **ow**-toh peh-**keh**-nyoh
I'd like a large car.	Quisiera un auto grande.	kee-**syeh**-rah oon **ow**-toh **grahn**-deh
I want a sports car.	Quiero un auto deportivo.	**kyeh**-roh oon **ow**-toh deh-pohr-**tee**-boh
I want an automatic.	Quiero un auto automático.	**kyeh**-roh oon **ow**-toh ow-toh-**mah**-tee-koh
What kind of gas does it take?	¿Qué tipo de gasolina necesita?	keh **tee**-poh deh gah-soh-**lee**-nah neh-seh-**see**-tah (Am) keh **tee**-poh deh gah-soh-**lee**-nah neh-theh-**see**-tah (Sp)
Is the gas included?	¿Está incluida la gasolina?	eh-**stah** een-**klwee**-dah lah gah-soh-**lee**-nah

English	Spanish	Pronunciation
How much does it cost...?	*¿Cuánto cuesta...?*	***kwahn**-toh **kweh**-stah*
per day	por día	pohr **dee**-ah
per week	por semana	pohr seh-**mah**-nah
per month	por mes	pohr mehs
Do I have to pay extra by kilometre?	¿Tengo que pagar más por kilómetro?	**tehn**-goh keh pah-**gahr** mahs pohr kee-**loh**-meh-troh
How much does it cost per kilometre?	¿Cuánto cuesta por kilómetro?	**kwahn**-toh **kweh**-stah pohr kee-**loh**-meh-troh
Does it include unlimited mileage?	¿Incluye kilometraje ilimitado?	een-**kloo**-yeh kee-loh-meh-**trah**-heh ee-lee-mee-**tah**-doh
How much is the insurance?	¿Cuánto cuesta el seguro?	**kwahn**-toh **kweh**-stah ehl seh-**goo**-roh
Do I have to return the car here?	¿Debo devolver el auto aquí?	**deh**-boh deh-bohl-**behr** ehl **ow**-toh ah-**kee**
Can I leave the car in...?	¿Puedo dejar el auto en...?	**pweh**-doh deh-**hahr** ehl **ow**-toh ehn
Here's my driver's licence.	Aquí está mi licencia para manejar. (Am)	ah-**kee** eh-**stah** mee lee-**sehn**-syah **pah**-rah mah-neh-**hahr** (Am)
	Aquí está mi permiso de conducir. (Sp)	ah-**kee** eh-**stah** mee pehr-**mee**-soh deh kohn-doo-**theer** (Sp)
I have an international driver's licence.	Tengo una licencia internacional.	**tehn**-goh **oo**-nah lee-**sehn**-syah een-tehr-nah-syoh-**nahl** (Am)
		tehn-goh **oo**-nah lee-**thehn**-thyah een-tehr-nah-thyoh-**nahl** (Sp)
Can I pay with my credit card?	¿Puedo pagar con mi tarjeta de crédito?	**pweh**-doh pah-**gahr** kohn mee tahr-**heh**-tah deh **kreh**-dee-toh

At the gas station

Gas stations are not as plentiful as in Canada and the U.S. As a result, you should always keep your tank fairly full. In Mexico, not every gas station offers unleaded gas. When you find one that does, make sure that your tank is full.

Where is there a gas station?	¿Dónde hay una bomba? (Am)	**dohn**-deh ahy **oo**-nah **bohm**-bah (Am)
	¿Dónde hay una gasolinera? (Sp)	**dohn**-deh ahy **oo**-nah gah-soh-lee-**neh**-rah (Sp)
Fill it up with...	*Llénelo con...*	***yeh**-neh-loh kohn (Am)*
		***lyeh**-neh-loh kohn (Sp)*
diesel	diesel	**dee**-sehl
regular	normal	nohr-**mahl**
extra	extra	**ehk**-strah (Am)
		eh-strah (Sp)
super	super	**soo**-pehr
Please check...	*Por favor, inspeccione...*	*pohr fah-**bohr** een-spehk-**syoh**-neh (Am)*
		*pohr fah-**bohr** een-spehk-**thyoh**-neh (Sp)*
the oil	el aceite	ehl ah-**say**-teh (Am)
		ehl ah-**thay**-teh (Sp)
the brake fluid	el líquido de frenos	ehl **lee**-kee-doh deh **freh**-nohs
the tire pressure	la presión de las llantas	lah preh-**syohn** deh lahs **yahn**-tahs (Am)
		lah preh-**syohn** deh lahs **lyahn**-tahs (Sp)
the battery	la batería	lah bah-teh-**ree**-ah
the antifreeze	el agua del radiador	ehl **ah**-gwah dehl rah-dyah-**dohr**
the transmission	la transmisión	lah trahns-mee-**syohn**
the carburetor	el carburador	ehl kahr-boo-rah-**dohr**
the fan belt	la correa del ventilador	lah koh-**rreh**-ah dehl behn-tee-lah-**dohr**
the exhaust	el escape	ehl eh-**skah**-peh

Car problems

Do you have a mechanic?	¿Tiene un mecánico?	**tyeh**-neh oon meh-**kah**-nee-koh
The car won't start.	El auto no arranca.	ehl **ow**-toh noh ah-**rrahn**-kah
I have a flat tire.	Tengo una llanta pinchada.	**tehn**-goh **oo**-nah **yahn**-tah peen-**chah**-dah (Am) **tehn**-goh **oo**-nah **lyahn**-tah peen-**chah**-dah (Sp)
The engine overheats.	El motor se calienta.	ehl moh-**tohr** seh kah-**lyehn**-tah
The car stalls.	El motor se para.	ehl moh-**tohr** seh **pah**-rah
I need a tow truck.	Necesito un carro de remolque.	neh-seh-**see**-toh oon **kah**-rroh deh rreh-**mohl**-keh (Am) neh-theh-**see**-toh oon **kah**-rroh deh rreh-**mohl**-keh (Sp)

On the road

Most roads and highways in Spain and Mexico are in excellent condition. Major highways are called **autopistas** in Spain and **carreteras** in Mexico and Latin America. Toll highways also exist in both Spain and Mexico. In Spain a toll highway is called an **autopista de peaje** and in Mexico, a **carretera cuota**. Speeds are always listed in kilometres. Radar is commonly used and you could be faced with a hefty fine if you try to keep up with the locals.

City driving can be a nightmare, especially if you're not familiar with the city. European cities often have a very different kind of urban planning than that which we find in North American cities. Streets don't always run in north-south, east-west directions. City blocks can have very irregular shapes. There are often many narrow, winding, one-way streets that require careful negotiating. Mexico City is one of the most populated cities, if not the most populated city on the planet. During business hours, the traffic is never ending.

Again, there are many one-way streets as well as traffic circles to deal with. There are also wide avenues with eight or more lanes of traffic. You might wisely leave your car at your hotel and get around town by using cabs or public transportation.

If you're a member of an automobile association (CAA or AAA), it would be smart to visit the association offices before you leave. They can provide you with maps, discount vouchers, charts explaining international road signs, as well as lots of useful hints.

north	el norte	ehl **nohr**-teh
south	el sud	ehl sood
east	el este	ehl **eh**-steh
west	el oeste	ehl oh-**eh**-steh
to the right	a la derecha	ah lah deh-**reh**-chah
to the left	a la izquierda	ah lah ees-**kyehr**-dah (Am) ah lah eeth-**kyehr**-dah (Sp)
straight ahead	todo recto	**toh**-doh **rrehk**-toh
	or	
	todo derecho	**toh**-doh deh-**reh**-choh

Here are some useful phrases that you can use while driving in and through Spanish-speaking countries:

Do you have a road map?	¿Tiene un mapa de carreteras? (Am)	**tyeh**-neh oon **mah**-pah deh kah-rreh-**teh**-rahs (Am)
	¿Tiene un mapa de autopistas? (Sp)	**tyeh**-neh oon **mah**-pah deh ow-toh-**pee**-stahs (Sp)
What's the speed limit?	¿Cuál es el límite de velocidad?	kwahl ehs ehl **lee**-mee-teh deh beh-loh-see-**dahd** (Am) kwahl ehs ehl **lee**-mee-teh deh beh-loh-thee-**dahd** (Sp)
How do I get to the main highway?	¿Cómo llego a la carretera principal? (Am)	**koh**-moh **yeh**-goh ah lah kah-rreh-**teh**-rah preen-see-**pahl** (Am)

How do I get to the main highway?	¿Cómo llego a la autopista principal? (Sp)	**koh**-moh **lyeh**-goh ah lah ow-toh-**pee**-stah preen-thee-**pahl** (Sp)
How do I get to...?	¿Cómo voy a...?	**koh**-moh boy ah
Is the road in good shape?	¿Está el camino en buenas condiciones?	eh-**stah** ehl kah-**mee**-noh ehn **bweh**-nahs kohn-dee-**syoh**-nehs (Am) eh-**stah** ehl kah-**mee**-noh ehn **bweh**-nahs kohn-dee-**thyoh**-nehs (Sp)
Is the road in bad shape?	¿Está el camino en malas condiciones?	eh-**stah** ehl kah-**mee**-noh ehn **mah**-lahs kohn-dee-**syoh**-nehs (Am) eh-**stah** ehl kah-**mee**-noh ehn **mah**-lahs kohn-dee-**thyoh**-nehs (Sp)
Do I go straight ahead?	¿Sigo todo recto?	**see**-goh **toh**-doh **rrehk**-toh
Do I turn right?	¿Voy a la derecha?	boy ah lah deh-**reh**-chah
Do I turn left?	¿Voy a la izquierda?	boy ah lah ees-**kyehr**-dah (Am) boy ah lah eeth-**kyehr**-dah (Sp)
How far away is...?	¿A qué distancia está...?	ah keh dee-**stahn**-syah eh-**stah** (Am) ah keh dee-**stahn**-thyah eh-**stah** (Sp)
Are there any detours?	¿Hay desviaciones?	ahy dehs-byah-**syoh**-nehs (Am) ahy dehs-byah-**thyoh**-nehs (Sp)
Is there a gas station nearby?	¿Hay una estación de gasolina cerca?	ahy **oo**-nah eh-stah-**syohn** deh gah-soh-**lee**-nah **sehr**-kah (Am) ahy **oo**-nah eh-stah-**thyohn** deh gah-soh-**lee**-nah **thehr**-kah (Sp)
Where are we?	¿Dónde estamos?	**dohn**-deh eh-**stah**-mohs

I think we're lost.	Creo que estamos perdidos.	**kreh**-oh keh eh-**stah**-mohs pehr-**dee**-dohs
Can you show me where I am on the map?	¿Puede indicarme en el mapa dónde estoy?	**pweh**-deh een-dee-**kahr**-meh ehn ehl **mah**-pah **dohn**-deh eh-**stoy**
Where can I park the car?	¿Dónde puedo parquear el auto? (Am)	**dohn**-deh **pweh**-doh pahr-keh-**ahr** ehl **ow**-toh (Am)
	¿Dónde puedo estacionar el auto? (Sp)	**dohn**-deh **pweh**-doh eh-stah-thyoh-**nahr** ehl **ow**-toh (Sp)
Can I park the car here?	¿Puedo parquear el auto aquí? (Am)	**pweh**-doh pahr-keh-**ahr** ehl **ow**-toh ah-**kee** (Am)
	¿Puedo estacionar el auto aquí?	**pweh**-doh eh-stah-thyoh-**nahr** ehl **ow**-toh ah-**kee** (Sp)

SIGN LANGUAGE

Here are some common road signs that you will see while travelling by car:

NO PARKING	NO ESTACIONAR
	ESTACIONAMIENTO PROHIBIDO
ONE WAY	DIRECCIÓN ÚNICA
DETOUR	DESVIACIÓN
	DESVÍO
PEDESTRIAN CROSSWALK	PASO DE PEATONES
STOP	ALTO
DANGER	PELIGRO

CHAPTER SEVEN

Sightseeing

The Spanish-speaking world is vast and offers you a wealth of sightseeing opportunities. Spain, the land of castles and monasteries, has been influenced by many cultures throughout its history. The Romans were the first to bring the civilized world to Spain. They built cities, roads, bridges and aqueducts that are still in evidence today. Don't miss the medieval city of Segovia with its aqueduct dating back to the first century A.D. and its **Alcázar**, a charming castle that looks like it was plucked from Walt Disney's *Sleeping Beauty*. Other cultures have also contributed to what is now Spain, including the Visigoths - Germanic tribes that travelled and settled throughout Europe, and the Moors - Arabs from Morocco who occupied Spain for more than seven centuries. The Moorish influence is evident in the south of Spain, especially in the cities of Granada, Córdoba and Sevilla. Don't miss the sultan's palace, the **Alhambra**, in Granada. Spain has large, world-class cities such as Madrid and Barcelona whose attractions rate a guidebook of their own. The former capital of Spain, Toledo, is a short trip from Madrid and well worth a day's visit. The entire city has been deemed an historic site. There are charming villages and beautiful beaches, as well churches, cathedrals, museums, art galleries, bullfights, gypsy flamenco shows and an active nightlife - all awaiting your visit.

The Spaniards conquered and colonized the New World. The area is so vast, it would be impossible to do justice here to the sights that are awaiting you. Certainly you don't want to miss the Archeological Museum in Mexico City which traces the history of Mexico's pre-Colombian cultures; the pyramids of the Sun and the Moon in Teotihuacán; as well as the many archeological ruins that are scattered throughout the country. Costa Rica, the Switzerland of the New World—Bogotá, Colombia, the Athens of South America—Buenos Aires, Argentina, the Paris of the New World—the islands of the Caribbean—Machu Picchu, Peru the lost city of the Incas—these and many more are ready for you to explore.

Keep in mind that this book is primarily a phrase book to help you get along in Spanish-speaking countries. Do yourself a favor and get your hands on a good guidebook that will take you to all the points of interest on your travels. The foreign embassies, consulates, tourist offices and your travel agent can help you as well.

Here are some phrases that you'll find useful while sightseeing:

Where's the tourist office?	¿ Dónde está la oficina de turismo?	**dohn**-deh eh-**stah** lah oh-fee-**see**-nah deh too-**rees**-moh (Am) **dohn**-deh eh-**stah** lah oh-fee-**thee**-nah deh too-**rees**-moh (Sp)
What are the points of interest?	¿Cuáles son los lugares de interés?	**kwah**-lehs sohn lohs loo-**gah**-rehs deh een-teh-**rehs**
Do you have an English-speaking guide?	¿Tiene un guía que hable inglés?	**tyeh**-neh oon **gee**-ah keh **ah**-bleh een-**glehs**
Where can I buy a guidebook?	¿Dónde puedo comprar una guía turística?	**dohn**-deh **pweh**-doh kohm-**prahr oo**-nah **gee**-ah too-**ree**-stee-kah
I'm lost. Can you show me where I am on this map?	Estoy perdido (a). ¿Puede indicarme en este mapa dónde estoy?	eh-**stoy** pehr-**dee**-doh (dah) **pweh**-deh een-dee-**kahr**-meh ehn **eh**-steh **mah**-pah **dohn**-deh eh-**stoy**
I want to visit...	*Quiero visitar...*	***kyeh**-roh bee-see-**tahr***
the art museum	el museo de arte	ehl moo-**seh**-oh deh **ahr**-teh
the beach	la playa	lah **plah**-yah
the botanical gardens	el jardín botánico	ehl hahr-**deen** boh-**tah**-nee-koh
the bullring	la plaza de toros	lah **plah**-sah deh **toh**-rohs (Am)

I want to visit...	*Quiero visitar...*	***kyeh**-roh bee-see-**tahr***
the bullring	la plaza de toros	lah **plah**-thah deh **toh**-rohs (Sp)
the castle	el castillo	ehl kah-**stee**-yoh (Am) ehl kah-**stee**-lyoh (Sp)
the cathedral	la catedral	lah kah-teh-**drahl**
the church	la iglesia	la ee-**gleh**-syah
the downtown area	el centro de la ciudad	ehl **sehn**-troh deh lah syoo-**dahd** (Am) ehl **thehn**-troh deh lah thyoo-**dahd** (Sp)
the main square	el Zócalo	ehl **soh**-kah-loh (Mexico)
	la plaza mayor	lah **plah**-sah mah-**yohr** (Am) lah **plah**-thah mah-**yohr** (Sp)
the market	el mercado	ehl mehr-**kah**-doh
the mosque	la mezquita	lah meh-**skee**-tah (Am) lah meh-**thkee**-tah (Sp)
the mountains	las montañas	lahs mohn-**tah**-nyahs
the museum	el museo	ehl moo-**seh**-oh
the old section of the city	la parte vieja de la ciudad	lah **pahr**-teh **byeh**-hah deh lah syoo-**dahd** (Am) lah **pahr**-teh **byeh**-hah deh lah thyoo-**dahd** (Sp)
the rainforest	la selva tropical	lah **sehl**-bah troh-peeh-**kahl**
the ruins	las ruinas	lahs **rrwee**-nahs
the stadium	el estadio	ehl eh-**stah**-dyoh
the synagogue	la sinagoga	lah see-nah-**goh**-gah
the university	la universidad	lah oo-nee-behr-see-**dahd**
the vineyards	las viñas	lahs **bee**-nyahs
the waterfall	la catarata	lah kah-tah-**rah**-tah
the zoo	el zoológico	ehl soh-**loh**-hee-koh (Am) ehl thoh-**loh**-hee-koh (Sp)
Can I take pictures?	¿Se puede sacar fotos?	seh **pweh**-deh sah-**kahr** **foh**-tohs
Where can I buy some postcards?	¿Dónde puedo comprar tarjetas postales?	**dohn**-deh **pweh**-doh kohm-**prahr** tahr-**heh**-tahs poh-**stah**-lehs

Is there a souvenir shop?	¿Hay una tienda de recuerdos?	ahy **oo**-nah **tyehn**-dah deh rreh-**kwehr**-dohs
What time do they open?	¿A qué hora se abre?	ah keh **oh**-rah seh **ah**-breh
What time do they close?	¿A qué hora se cierra?	ah keh **oh**-rah seh **syeh**-rrah (Am) ah keh **oh**-rah seh **thyeh**-rrah (Sp)
How much does it cost to get in?	¿Cuánto es la entrada?	**kwahn**-toh ehs lah ehn-**trah**-dah

It is customary to tip your guide if you've enjoyed your excursion. A good guide can make your outing an enjoyable and educational experience, so a 10 to 15 percent tip (the equivalent of two dollars or so) is money well spent.

SIGN LANGUAGE

TICKETS	BOLETOS (Am) BILLETES (Sp)	ENTRADAS (Sp)
TICKET WINDOW	BOLETERÍA (Am)	TAQUILLA (Sp)
ENTRANCE	ENTRADA	
EXIT	SALIDA	
OPEN	ABIERTO	
CLOSED	CERRADO	
WATCH OUT	CUIDADO	
NO SMOKING	NO FUMAR	
NO PICTURES ALLOWED	PROHIBIDO SACAR FOTOS	
DO NOT ENTER	NO HAY PASO	
DO NOT TOUCH	NO TOCAR	
DANGER	PELIGRO	

CHAPTER EIGHT

Dining out

Dining out in Spanish-speaking countries offers you an array of food that is so varied that you could eat for years and never have the same thing twice.

Spain is a peninsula that is surrounded on three sides by water, the Mediterranean, the Atlantic and the Bay of Biscay. As a result, Spain is known for its fish and seafood dishes. Roast suckling pig, roast lamb and rabbit are also on the menus of many fine Spanish restaurants. There are also regional dishes - **comida típica** - that are typical of the different areas in Spain. North American tourists are probably most familiar with **gazpacho**, a cold and refreshing tomato-based soup as well as **paella**, a rice dish served with chicken and seafood. Restaurants in Spain are rated from a five-fork (luxury) establishment down to a one-fork (cheerful and cheap) establishment. Most Spanish restaurants post their menus outside, so it's easy for you to find something that suits your pocketbook and tastes.

The Spaniards left their influence on the many different cuisines of Latin America. One dish that seems universal throughout the Spanish-speaking world is rice with chicken, even though the way in which the dish is presented can vary greatly from country to country. In addition, Latin American cuisine has been heavily influenced by native-Indian foods. Mexican and Latin American cuisine is often very hot and spicy (**picante**), since a variety of chilies is used in the preparation of many dishes. Beans form an important part of the Latin American diet as well. There are also many tortilla-based dishes throughout Mexico and Latin America. Tortillas can be made from corn or wheat flour and often replace bread and rolls. Some of the tortilla dishes that would be familiar to North Americans are **tacos**, **loros**, **pupusas**, **enchiladas**, **burritos**, **quesadillas** and **flautas**. Much of Mexico and Latin America are close to tropical waters. As a result, there is an abundance of fish and seafood that is particular to this area of the world. Tropical fruits and juices also abound throughout Latin America.

North American culture has reared its head in many Spanish-speaking countries. North American fast food chains (hamburger, fries and pizza palaces) are sprouting up everywhere and offer familiar fare to tourists who lack the daring to try the typical dishes of the countries that they are visiting.

In Spanish-speaking countries, many businesses close between 2:00 and 4:00 p.m. (**siesta**) so that their employees may go home for their main meal of the day - the lunchtime meal. As a tourist, you should be aware that the evening meal in Spain is served quite late. It's not unusual to have your evening meal at 10:00 p.m. or later. Spain has an active nightlife that begins around 11:00 p.m. and goes on until dawn. Spaniards are used to eating very late. However, you can find some restaurants that cater to North American customs and will offer you your evening meal earlier.

Wherever you go in the Spanish-speaking world, a veritable feast awaits you. Be adventurous and try something new. However, be wise and always eat in clean, well-established restaurants in order to avoid stomach upsets. Always drink bottled water. Even though many hotels and restaurants may claim that their water is purified, it's not worth the risk of having to suffer "turista" stomach. Remember to order your drinks "without ice" (**sin hielo** - seen **yeh**-loh). Many tourists have taken all the necessary precautions to avoid stomach upsets and have still suffered because they forgot about the ice. The same applies to the hot, spicy foods that abound in Mexico and parts of Latin America. Unless you have a cast-iron stomach, avoid purchasing food from street vendors, even though the wonderful aromas make your mouth salivate.

Many restaurants will include "service" on the bill. It is usually 10 to 15 percent of the bill and it is not optional. If your waiter's service is exceptional, you may want to leave a bit more to show your gratitude.

In order to get your server's attention, never snap your fingers. In Mexico, you can raise your hand and call out "**mesero**" for a male, or "**mesera**" for a female. In Spain, you would address your waiter as "**mozo**" or "**camarero**" and your waitress as "**señorita**" or "**camarera**." Another way to get their attention is to raise your hand and say, "**por favor**" at an opportune time.

Can you recommend a typical restaurant?	¿Puede recomendar un restaurante típico?	**pweh**-deh rreh-koh-mehn-**dahr** oon rreh-stow-**rahn**-teh **tee**-pee-koh
Can you recommend a restaurant for...?	*¿Puede recomendar un restaurante para...?*	***pweh**-deh rreh-koh-mehn-**dahr** oon rreh-stow-**rahn**-teh **pah**-rah*
breakfast	el desayuno	ehl deh-sah-**yoo**-noh
lunch	el almuerzo (Am) la comida (Sp)	ehl ahl-**mwehr**-soh (Am) lah koh-**mee**-dah (Sp)
dinner	la cena	lah **seh**-nah (Am) lah **theh**-nah (Sp)
I'd like to reserve a table...	*Quisiera reservar una mesa...*	*kee-**syeh**-rah rreh-sehr-**bahr** **oo**-nah **meh**-sah*
for today	para hoy	**pah**-rah oy
for tonight	para esta noche	**pah**-rah **eh**-stah **noh**-cheh
for tomorrow	para mañana	**pah**-rah mah-**nyah**-nah
for two (people)	para dos	**pah**-rah dohs.
for nine o'clock	para las nueve	**pah**-rah lahs **nweh**-beh

We have a reservation for 10 o'clock.	Tenemos una reservación para las diez. (Am)	teh-**neh**-mohs **oo**-nah rreh-sehr-bah-**syohn** **pah**-rah lahs dyehs (Am)
	Tenemos una reserva para las diez. (Sp)	teh-**neh**-mohs **oo**-nah rreh-**sehr**-bah **pah**-rah lahs dyehth (Sp)
Bring me...please.	*Tráigame...por favor.*	***trahy**-gah-meh pohr fah-**bohr***
the menu	la carta	lah **kahr**-tah
the wine list	la carta de vinos	lah **kahr**-tah deh **bee**-nohs
an aperitif	un aperitivo	oon ah-peh-ree-**tee**-boh
a cocktail	un coctel	oon kohk-**tehl**
a glass of red wine	una copa de vino tinto	**oo**-nah **koh**-pah deh **bee**-noh **teen**-toh
a glass of white wine	una copa de vino blanco	**oo**-nah **koh**-pah deh **bee**-noh **blahn**-koh
a jug of sangria	un jarro de sangría	oon **hah**-rroh deh sahn-**gree**-ah
a bottle of mineral water with (without) gas	una botella de agua mineral con (sin) gas	**oo**-nah boh-**teh**-yah deh **ah**-gwah mee-neh-**rahl** kohn (seen) gahs (Am)
		oo-nah boh-**teh**-lyah deh **ah**-gwah mee-neh-**rahl** kohn (seen) gahs (Sp)
a beer	una cerveza	**oo**-nah sehr-**beh**-sah (Am)
		oo-nah thehr-**beh**-thah (Sp)
What's the house wine?	¿Cuál es el vino de la casa?	kwahl ehs ehl **bee**-noh deh lah **kah**-sah
What's the house specialty?	¿Cuál es la especialidad de la casa?	kwahl ehs lah eh-speh-syah-lee-**dahd** deh lah **kah**-sah (Am)
		kwahl ehs lah eh-speh-thyah-lee-**dahd** deh lah **kah**-sah (Sp)

We're ready to order.	Estamos listos para pedir.	eh-**stah**-mohs **lee**-stohs **pah**-rah peh-**deer**
I like the meat...	*Me gusta la carne...*	*meh **goo**-stah lah **kahr**-neh*
rare	poco cocida	**poh**-koh koh-**see**-dah (Am) **poh**-koh koh-**thee**-dah (Sp)
medium	mediana	meh-**dyah**-nah
well done	bien cocida.	byehn koh-**see**-dah (Am) byehn koh-**thee**-dah (Sp)
I need...	*Necesito...*	*neh-seh-**see**-toh (Am)* *neh-theh-**see**-toh (Sp)*
a fork	un tenedor	oon teh-neh-**dohr**
a teaspoon	una cucharita	**oo**-nah koo-chah-**ree**-tah
a spoon	una cuchara	**oo**-nah koo-**chah**-rah
a knife	un cuchillo	oon koo-**chee**-yoh (Am) oon koo-**chee**-lyoh (Sp)
a napkin	una servilleta	**oo**-nah sehr-bee-**yeh**-tah (Am) **oo**-nah sehr-bee-**lyeh**-tah (Sp)
Where's the toilet?	¿Dónde está el servicio? (Am) ¿Dónde está el aseo? (Sp)	**dohn**-deh eh-**stah** ehl sehr-**bee**-syoh (Am) **dohn**-deh eh-**stah** ehl ah-**seh**-oh (Sp)
Is the service included?	¿Está incluido el servicio?	eh-**stah** een-**klwee**-doh ehl sehr-**bee**-syoh (Am) eh-**stah** een-**klwee**-doh ehl sehr-**bee**-thyoh (Sp)
The cheque, please.	La cuenta, por favor.	lah **kwehn**-tah pohr fah-**bohr**
Excuse me, there's a mistake.	Perdón, hay un error.	pehr-**dohn** ahy oon eh-**rrohr**

MINI DICTIONARY

Breakfast

bacon and eggs	huevos con tocino	**weh**-bohs kohn toh-**see**-noh (Am) **weh**-bohs kohn toh-**thee**-noh (Sp)
ham and eggs	huevos con jamón	**weh**-bohs kohn hah-**mohn**
eggs...	*huevos...*	***weh**-bohs*
scrambled	revueltos	rreh-**bwehl**-tohs
fried	fritos	**free**-tohs
boiled	pasados por agua	pah-**sah**-dohs pohr **ah**-gwah
soft-boiled	tibios	**tee**-byohs
hard-boiled	duros	**doo**-rohs
4-minute eggs	pasados por agua, cuatro minutos	pah-**sah**-dohs pohr **ah**-gwah **kwah**-troh mee-**noo**-tohs
poached	escalfados	eh-skahl-**fah**-dohs
an omelette	una tortilla	**oo**-nah tohr-**tee**-yah (Am) **oo**-nah tohr-**tee**-lyah (Sp)
a sweet roll	un pan dulce	oon pahn **dool**-seh (Am) oon pahn **dool**-theh (Sp)
rolls	panecillos	pah-neh-**see**-yohs (Am) pah-neh-**thee**-lyohs (Sp)
toast	pan tostado	pahn toh-**stah**-doh
jam, marmalade	mermelada	mehr-meh-**lah**-dah
butter	manteca (Am) mantequilla (Sp)	mahn-**teh**-kah (Am) mahn-teh-**kee**-lyah (Sp)
margarine	margarina	mahr-gah-**ree**-nah
hot cereal	cereal cocido	seh-reh-**ahl** koh-**see**-doh (Am) theh-reh-**ahl** koh-**thee**-doh (Sp)
stewed prunes	ciruelas pasas	seer-**weh**-lahs **pah**-sahs (Am) theer-**weh**-lahs **pah**-sahs (Sp)

Drinks

orange juice	jugo de naranja (Am)	**hoo**-goh deh nah-**rahn**-hah (Am)
	zumo de naranja (Sp)	**thoo**-moh deh nah-**rahn**-hah (Sp)
apple juice	jugo de manzana (Am)	**hoo**-goh deh mahn-**sah**-nah (Am)
	zumo de manzana (Sp)	**thoo**-moh deh mahn-**thah**-nah (Sp)
tomato juice	jugo de tomate (Am)	**hoo**-goh deh toh-**mah**-teh (Am)
	zumo de tomate (Sp)	**thoo**-moh deh toh-**mah**-teh (Sp)
grapefruit juice	jugo de toronja (Am)	**hoo**-goh deh toh-**rohn**-hah (Am)
	zumo de pomelo (Sp)	**thoo**-moh deh poh-**meh**-loh (Sp)
black coffee	café solo	kah-**feh soh**-loh
coffee with cream	café con crema	kah-**feh** kohn **kreh**-mah
coffee with milk (North American coffee)	un cortado	oon kohr-**tah**-doh
half coffee, half hot milk	café con leche	kah-**feh** kohn **leh**-cheh
decaffeinated coffee	café sin cafeína	kah-**feh** seen kah-feh-**ee**-nah
tea...	*té...*	*teh*
with milk	con leche	kohn **leh**-cheh
with lemon	con limón	kohn lee-**mohn**
with sugar	con azúcar	kohn ah-**soo**-kahr (Am) kohn ah-**thoo**-kahr (Sp)
with sweetner	con sacarina	kohn sah-kah-**ree**-nah
a glass of milk	un vaso de leche	oon **bah**-soh deh **leh**-cheh
skimmed milk	leche desnatada	**leh**-cheh dehs-nah-**tah**-dah
hot chocolate	chocolate caliente	choh-koh-**lah**-teh kah-**lyehn**-teh

a milkshake	un batido	oon bah-**tee**-doh
a bottle of mineral water with (without) gas	una botella de agua mineral con (sin) gas	**oo**-nah boh-**teh**-yah deh **ah**-gwah mee-neh-**rahl** kohn (seen) gahs (Am) **oo**-nah boh-**teh**-lyah deh **ah**-gwah mee-neh-**rahl** kohn (seen) gahs (Sp)
a soft drink	un refresco (Am) una gaseosa (Sp)	oon rreh-**freh**-skoh (Am) **oo**-nah gah-seh-**oh**-sah (Sp)
a lemonade	una limonada	**oo**-nah lee-moh-**nah**-dah
a coke	una coca cola	**oo**-nah **koh**-kah **koh**-lah
a beer	una cerveza	**oo**-nah sehr-**beh**-sah (Am) **oo**-nah thehr-**beh**-thah (Sp)
white wine	vino blanco	**bee**-noh **blahn**-koh
red wine	vino tinto	**bee**-noh **teen**-toh
rosé	vino rosado	**bee**-noh rroh-**sah**-doh
whisky	whisky	**wee**-skee
gin and tonic	gin tonic	heen **toh**-neek
vodka	vodka	**bohd**-kah

Soups

consommé	consomé	kohn-soh-**meh**
gazpacho	gazpacho	gah-**spah**-choh (Am) gah-**thpah**-choh (Sp)
chicken soup	sopa de pollo	**soh**-pah deh **poh**-yoh (Am) **soh**-pah deh **poh**-lyoh (Sp)
fish soup	sopa de pescado	**soh**-pah deh peh-**skah**-doh
garlic soup	sopa de ajo	**soh**-pah deh **ah**-hoh
vegetable soup	sopa de legumbres	**soh**-pah deh leh-**goom**-brehs

Salads

a green salad	una ensalada verde	**oo**-nah ehn-sah-**lah**-dah **behr**-deh
a tomato salad	una ensalada de tomates	**oo**-nah ehn-sah-**lah**-dah deh toh-**mah**-tehs

salad dressing	aderezo	ah-deh-**reh**-soh (Am)
	vinagreta	bee-nah-**greh**-tah (Sp)

Meats

beef	carne de res	**kahr**-neh deh rehs
lamb	carne de cordero	**kahr**-neh deh kohr-**deh**-roh
pork	carne de cerdo	**kahr**-neh deh **sehr**-doh (Am) **kahr**-neh deh **thehr**-doh (Sp)
veal	carne de ternera	**kahr**-neh deh tehr-**neh**-rah
rabbit	conejo	koh-**neh**-hoh
steak	bistec	bee-**stehk**
hamburger	una hamburgesa	ahm-boor-**geh**-sah
roast beef	rosbif	rrohs-**beef**
chops	chuletas	choo-**leh**-tahs
ham	jamón	hah-**mohn**
liver	hígado	**ee**-gah-doh
sausage	salchicha	sahl-**chee**-chah

Poultry

chicken	pollo	**poh**-yoh (Am) **poh**-lyoh (Sp)
fried chicken	pollo frito	**poh**-yoh **free**-toh (Am) **poh**-lyoh **free**-toh (Sp)
grilled (broiled) chicken	pollo a la parilla	**poh**-yoh ah lah pah-**ree**-yah (Am) **poh**-lyoh ah lah pah-**ree**-lyah (Sp)
turkey	pavo	**pah**-boh
duck	pato	**pah**-toh
squab	pichón	pee-**chohn**

Fish and Seafood

salmon	salmón	sahl-**mohn**
tuna	atún	ah-**toon**
monkfish	rape	**rrah**-peh
cod	bacalao	bah-kah-**lah**-oh
bass	merluza	mehr-**loo**-sah (Am) mehr-**loo**-thah (Sp)
trout	trucha	**troo**-chah
shrimp	camarones	kah-mah-**roh**-nehs
shrimp (large)	gambas	**gahm**-bahs
squid	calamares	kah-lah-**mah**-rehs
mussels	mejillones	meh-hee-**yoh**-nehs (Am) meh-hee-**lyoh**-nehs (Sp)
oysters	ostras	**oh**-strahs
snails	caracoles	kah-rah-**koh**-lehs
lobster	langosta	lahn-**goh**-stah
shellfish stew	zarzuela de mariscos	sahr-**sweh**-lah deh mah-**rees**-kohs (Am) thahr-**thweh**-lah deh mah-**rees**-kohs (Sp)

Pasta and Rice

spaghetti with meatballs	fideos con albóndigas	fee-**deh**-ohs kohn ahl-**bohn**-dee-gahs
rice with saffron	arroz con azafrán	ah-**rrohs** kohn ah-sah-**frahn** (Am) ah-**rrohth** kohn ah-thah-**frahn** (Sp)
chicken and rice	arroz con pollo	ah-**rrohs** kohn **poh**-yoh (Am) ah-**rrohth** kohn **poh**-lyoh (Sp)
paella (saffron rice with chicken and seafood)	paella	pah-**eh**-yah (Am) pah-**eh**-lyah (Sp)

Be careful when ordering raw vegetables. You can't always be sure that they were washed using purified water. Tourists can suffer severe bouts of diarrhea after eating food that has not been carefully prepared. Some of the bacteria found in raw fruits and vegetables can cause you stomach disorders long after your return from you holiday.

Vegetables

artichokes	alcachofas	ahl-kah-**choh**-fahs
asparagus	espárragos	eh-**spah**-rrah-gohs
avocado	aguacate	ah-gwah-**kah**-teh
beans (refried)	frijoles	free-**hoh**-lehs
broccoli	brécol	**breh**-kohl
carrots	zanahorias	sah-nah-**oh**-ryahs (Am) thah-nah-**oh**-ryahs (Sp)
cauliflower	coliflor	koh-lee-**flohr**
corn	maíz	mah-**ees** (Am) mah-**eeth** (Sp)
eggplant	berenjena	beh-rehn-**heh**-nah
green beans	judías verdes	hoo-**dee**-ahs **behr**-dehs
peas	arbejas (Am) guisantes (Sp)	ahr-**beh**-hahs (Am) gee-**sahn**-tehs (Sp)
spinach	espinacas	eh-spee-**nah**-kahs
French fries	papas fritas (Am) patatas fritas (Sp)	**pah**-pahs **free**-tahs (Am) pah-**tah**-tahs **free**-tahs (Sp)
mashed potatoes	puré de papas (Am) puré de patatas (Sp)	poo-**reh** deh **pah**-pahs (Am) poo-**reh** deh pah-**tah**-tahs (Sp)
baked potatoes	papas al horno (Am) patatas al horno (Sp)	**pah**-pahs ahl **ohr**-noh (Am) pah-**tah**-tahs ahl **ohr**-noh (Sp)

boiled potatoes	papas hervidas (Am)	**pah**-pahs ehr-**bee**-dahs (Am)
	patatas hervidas (Sp)	pah-**tah**-tahs ehr-**bee**-dahs (Sp)

Corn **(maíz)** plays an important role in Mexican and Latin American cuisine. However, in Spain corn is normally used as fodder for animals.

Condiments

salt	sal	sahl
pepper	pimienta	pee-**myehn**-tah
ketchup	salsa de tomate	**sahl**-sah deh toh-**mah**-teh
mustard	mostaza	moh-**stah**-sah (Am) moh-**stah**-thah (Sp)
mayonnaise	mayonesa	mah-yoh-**neh**-sah
vinegar	vinagre	bee-**nah**-greh
oil	aceite	ah-**say**-teh (Am) ah-**thay**-teh (Sp)

Fruits and Desserts

apple	manzana	mahn-**sah**-nah (Am) mahn-**thah**-nah (Sp)
banana	banana (Am)	bah-**nah**-nah (Am)
	plátano (Sp)	**plah**-tah-noh (Sp)
cherry	cereza	seh-**reh**-sah (Am) theh-**reh**-thah (Sp)
grapes	uvas	**oo**-bahs
lemon	limón	lee-**mohn**
lime	lima	**lee**-mah
melon	melón	meh-**lohn**
orange	naranja	nah-**rahn**-hah
peach	durazno (Am)	doo-**rah**-snoh (Am)
	melocotón (Sp)	meh-loh-koh-**tohn**
pear	pera	**peh**-rah

pineapple	ananás (Am)	ah-nah-**nahs** (Am)
	piña (Sp)	**pee**-nyah (Sp)
plum	ciruela	seer-**weh**-lah (Am)
		theer-**weh**-lah (Sp)
raspberry	frambuesa	frahm-**bweh**-sah
strawberry	frutilla (Am)	froo-**tee**-yah (Am)
	fresa (Sp)	**freh**-sah (Sp)
watermelon	sandía	sahn-**dee**-ah
rice pudding	arroz con leche	ah-**rrohs** kohn **leh**-cheh (Am)
		ah-**rrohth** kohn **leh**-cheh (Sp)
caramel custard	flan	flahn
cake	pastel	pah-**stehl**
pie	torta	**tohr**-tah
fruit tart	tarta	**tahr**-tah
cookies	galletas	gah-**yeh**-tahs (Am)
		gah-**lyeh**-tahs (Sp)
ice cream...	*helado...*	*eh-**lah**-doh*
chocolate	de chocolate	deh choh-koh-**lah**-teh
vanilla	de vainilla	deh bahy-**nee**-yah (Am)
		deh bahy-**nee**-lyah (Sp)
cheese	queso	**keh**-soh

CHAPTER NINE

Shopping

Spanish-speaking countries offer you a range of commodities from world-class products to regional and local items. You can shop in large department stores similar to those found in Canada, in smaller shops and boutiques, in flea markets or from street vendors. Be aware that many businesses close between 2:00 and 4:00 p.m. for **siesta**. However, in larger cities major department stores and international businesses remain open throughout the afternoon.

In Spain, there are several chains of department stores - you'll even find Sears in Madrid - and these are a good source of quality products. There are also handicraft stores called **Artespaña** (ahr-teh-**spah**-nyah) which carry products from the different regions of the country. These stores are found throughout Spain.

Bargaining is a fairly common activity in Mexico and throughout Latin America. In fact, you are expected to bargain in the open-air markets and with street vendors who sell everything from compact discs to hammocks. In Spain, you may bargain at flea markets such as Madrid's Rastro market but generally a shopper pays the price advertised. The same applies to large department stores and shops in Mexico and Latin America.

Spain is known for leather goods, lace and embroidery, fans and combs, pearls, pottery, handicrafts and jewellery, as well as knives and swords. Mexico and Latin America offer silver items, woven fabrics, rugs, pottery, figurines, papier-mâché products, bark paintings, as well as many handicrafts particular to each region.

When shopping in markets, take your time to go from vendor to vendor to compare prices. Don't appear too interested and then return to the vendor with the lowest price. If you have your heart set on a particular item, the vendor will recognize this and there won't be much room for bargaining. You have to be prepared to walk away. The vendor will call you back if there's still room to negotiate.

If you're planning to purchase video cassettes, remember that Europe operates on a different system from that of North America. Any tapes that you purchase in Spain will not run on our VCRs. Audio cassettes and compact discs do not pose a problem. If you're in the market for electronic equipment, keep in mind that some products may not be compatible with our system. In addition, the warranties on these products may not be valid in Canada.

Enjoy your shopping adventures but don't forget that you must declare your purchases upon your return to Canada. Keep all of your receipts in order to avoid problems when clearing Canadian customs.

Perdón, buenos días, por favor, muchas gracias and a friendly smile work wonders when making purchases and when bargaining.

Where is there...?	*¿Dónde hay...?*	***dohn**-deh ahy*
a bakery	una panadería	**oo**-nah pah-nah-deh-**ree**-ah
a bookstore	una librería	**oo**-nah lee-breh-**ree**-ah
a camera shop	una tienda de artículos fotográficos	**oo**-nah **tyehn**-dah deh ahr-**tee**-koo-lohs foh-toh-**grah**-fee-kohs
a clothing store	una tienda de ropa	**oo**-nah **tyehn**-dah deh **rroh**-pah
a department store	un almacén	oon ahl-mah-**sehn** (Am) oon ahl-mah-**thehn** (Sp)
a drugstore	una farmacia	**oo**-nah fahr-**mah**-syah (Am) **oo**-nah fahr-**mah**-thyah (Sp)
a gift shop	una tienda de regalos	**oo**-nah **tyehn**-dah deh rreh-**gah**-lohs

a grocery store	una tienda de comestibles	**oo**-nah **tyehn**-dah deh koh-meh-**stee**-blehs
a jewellery store	una joyería	**oo**-nah hoh-yeh-**ree**-ah
a liquor store	una licorería	**oo**-nah lee-koh-reh-**ree**-ah
a market	un mercado	oon mehr-**kah**-doh
a newsstand	un puesto de periódicos	oon **pweh**-stoh deh peh-**ryoh**-dee-kohs
a record store	una tienda de discos	**oo**-nah **tyehn**-dah deh **dees**-kohs
a shoe store	una zapatería	**oo**-nah sah-pah-teh-**ree**-ah (Am) **oo**-nah thah-pah-teh-**ree**-ah (Sp)
a shoemaker	un zapatero	oon sah-pah-**teh**-roh (Am) oon thah-pah-**teh**-roh (Sp)
a supermarket	un supermercado	oon soo-pehr-mehr-**kah**-doh
a tailor shop	una sastrería	**oo**-nah sah-streh-**ree**-ah
a watchmaker	un relojero	oon rreh-loh-**heh**-roh
Can you help me?	¿Puede ayudarme?	**pweh**-deh ah-yoo-**dahr**-meh

CLOTHING

I want to buy...	*Quiero comprar...*	***kyeh**-roh kohm-**prahr***
a bathing cap	un gorro de baño	oon **goh**-rroh deh **bah**-nyoh
a bathing suit	un traje de baño	oon **trah**-heh deh **bah**-nyoh
a bathrobe	una bata	**oo**-nah **bah**-tah
a belt	un cinturón	oon seen-too-**rohn** (Am) oon theen-too-**rohn** (Sp)
a blouse	una blusa	**oo**-nah **bloo**-sah
a brassiere	un sostén	oon soh-**stehn**
a cap	una gorra	**oo**-nah **goh**-rrah
a dress	un vestido	oon beh-**stee**-doh
an evening dress	un traje de noche	oon **trah**-heh deh **noh**-cheh
a hat	un sombrero	oon sohm-**breh**-roh
a jacket	una chaqueta	**oo**-nah chah-**keh**-tah
an overcoat	un abrigo	oon ah-**bree**-goh
a nightgown	una camisa de noche	**oo**-nah kah-**mee**-sah deh **noh**-cheh

I want to buy...	*Quiero comprar...*	***kyeh**-roh kohm-**prahr***
a pair of boots	un par de botas	oon pahr deh **boh**-tahs
a pair of gloves	un par de guantes	oon pahr deh **gwahn**-tehs
a pair of jeans	un par de jeans	oon pahr deh jeens
a pair of pants	pantalones	pahn-tah-**loh**-nehs
a pair of shoes	un par de zapatos	oon pahr deh sah-**pah**-tohs (Am)
		oon pahr deh thah-**pah**-tohs (Sp)
a pair of shorts	pantalones cortos	pahn-tah-**loh**-nehs **kohr**-tohs
a pair of slippers	un par de zapatillas	oon pahr de sah-pah-**tee**-yahs (Am)
		oon pahr de thah-pah-**tee**-lyahs (Sp)
a pair of socks	calcetines	kahl-seh-**tee**-nehs (Am)
		kahl-theh-**tee**-nehs (Sp)
pantyhose	pantimedias	pahn-tee-**meh**-dyahs
pyjamas	un piyama (Am)	oon pee-**yah**-mah (Am)
	un pijama (Sp)	oon pee-**hah**-mah (Sp)
a raincoat	un impermeable	oon eem-pehr-meh-**ah**-bleh
rubber boots	zapatos de goma	sah-**pah**-tohs deh **goh**-mah (Am)
		thah-**pah**-tohs deh **goh**-mah (Sp)
a shirt	una camisa	**oo**-nah kah-**mee**-sah
a skirt	una falda	**oo**-nah **fahl**-dah
stockings	medias	**meh**-dyahs
a scarf	una bufanda	**oo**-nah boo-**fahn**-dah
a sweater	un suéter	oon **sweh**-tehr
a suit	un traje	oon **trah**-heh
a T-shirt	una camiseta	**oo**-nah kah-mee-**seh**-tah
a tie	una corbata	**oo**-nah kohr-**bah**-tah
an umbrella	un paraguas	oon pah-**rah**-gwahs
underwear	ropa interior	**rroh**-pah een-tehr-**yohr**
a windbreaker	un saco (Am)	oon **sah**-koh (Am)
	una chaqueta (Sp)	**oo**-nah chah-**keh**-tah (Sp)

Colours

I want it in...	*Lo quiero en...*	*loh **kyeh**-roh ehn*
black	negro	**neh**-groh
blue	azul	ah-**sool** (Am)
		ah-**thool** (Sp)
brown	marrón	mah-**rrohn**
gray	gris	grees
green	verde	**behr**-deh
orange	anaranjado	ah-nah-rahn-**hah**-doh
pink	rosado	rroh-**sah**-doh
purple	morado	moh-**rah**-doh
red	rojo	**rroh**-hoh
white	blanco	**blahn**-koh
yellow	amarillo	ah-mah-**ree**-yoh (Am)
		ah-mah-**ree**-lyoh (Sp)
I want a darker shade.	Quiero un tono más oscuro.	**kyeh**-roh oon **toh**-noh mahs oh-**skoo**-roh
I want a lighter shade.	Quiero un tono más claro.	**kyeh**-roh oon **toh**-noh mahs **klah**-roh

Fabrics

I want something in...	*Quiero algo en...*	***kyeh**-roh **ahl**-goh ehn*
cotton	algodón	ahl-goh-**dohn**
denim	dril de algodón	dreel deh ahl-goh-**dohn**
leather	cuero	**kweh**-roh
linen	hilo	**ee**-loh
nylon	nilón	nee-**lohn**
rayon	rayón	rrah-**yohn**
satin	raso	**rrah**-soh
silk	seda	**seh**-dah
suede	ante	**ahn**-teh
wool	lana	**lah**-nah

Sizes

I take size...	*Mi talla es...*	*mee **tah**-yah ehs (Am)* *mee **tah**-lyah ehs (Sp)*
small	pequeña	peh-**keh**-nyah or
	chica	**chee**-kah
medium	mediana	meh-**dyah**-nah
large	grande	**grahn**-deh
extra large	extra grande	**ehk**-strah **grahn**-deh (Am) **eh**-strah **grahn**-deh (Sp)
Do you have shoes in my size?	¿Tiene zapatos en mi tamaño?	**tyeh**-neh sah-**pah**-tohs ehn mee tah-**mah**-nyoh (Am) **tyeh**-neh thah-**pah**-tohs ehn mee tah-**mah**-nyoh (Sp)
Do you have something bigger?	¿Tiene algo más grande?	**tyeh**-neh **ahl**-goh mahs **grahn**-deh
Do you have something smaller?	¿Tiene algo más pequeño?	**tyeh**-neh **ahl**-goh mahs peh-**keh**-nyoh

Note that the word **talla** is used for "size" when referring to clothing and the word **tamaño** is used when referring to footwear.

CONVERSION CHART FOR CLOTHING AND SHOE SIZES

Men's dress shirts

Canada	14	14.5	15	15.5	16	16.5	17	17.5	18
Spain	36	37	38	39	41	42	43	44	45
Mexico	(may be the same as the Canadian or the Spanish sizes)								

Men's suits, jackets and coats

Canada and Mexico	36	38	40	42	44	46	48
Spain	46	48	50	52	54	56	58

Men's shoes

Canada	7	7.5	8	8.5	9	9.5	10	10.5	11	11.5	12
Mexico	6	6.5	7	7.5	8	8.5	9	9.5	10	10.5	11
Spain	39	40	41	42	43	44	45	46	47	48	49

Women's blouses and sweaters

Canada	small	medium	large
Mexico and Spain	chico	mediano	grande

Women's dresses, jackets and coats

Canada	6	8	10	12	14	16	18	20
Mexico	30	32	34	36	38	40	42	44
Spain	34	36	38	40	42	44	46	48

Women's shoes

Canada	5	6	7	8	9	10	11
Mexico	2	3	4	5	6	7	8
Spain	36	37	38	39	40	41	42

Additional phrases

I like this one.	Me gusta ésta.	meh **goo**-stah **eh**-stah
I like these.	Me gustan éstas.	meh **goo**-stahn **eh**-stahs
How much does it cost?	¿Cuánto cuesta?	**kwahn**-toh **kweh**-stah
How much do they cost?	¿Cuánto cuestan?	**kwahn**-toh **kweh**-stahn

Do you have something cheaper?	¿Tiene algo más barato?	**tyeh**-neh **ahl**-goh mahs bah-**rah**-toh
Do you have something more expensive?	¿Tiene algo más caro?	**tyeh**-neh **ahl**-goh mahs **kah**-roh
May I try it on?	¿Puedo probármelo?	**pweh**-doh proh-**bahr**-meh-loh
Where are the change rooms, please?	¿Dónde están los vestuarios, por favor?	**dohn**-deh eh-**stahn** lohs beh-**stwah**-ryohs pohr fah-**bohr**
It doesn't fit me.	No me queda bien.	noh meh **keh**-dah byehn
It's a good fit.	Me queda bien.	meh **keh**-dah byehn
I'll take it.	Me lo llevo.	meh loh **yeh**-boh (Am) meh loh **lyeh**-boh (Sp)
Where should I pay?	¿Dónde debo pagar?	**dohn**-deh **deh**-boh pah-**gahr**
Do your take traveller's cheques?	¿Acepta cheques de viajero?	ah-**sehp**-tah **cheh**-kehs deh byah-**heh**-roh (Am) ah-**thehp**-tah **cheh**-kehs deh byah-**heh**-roh (Sp)
I need a receipt.	Necesito un recibo.	neh-seh-**see**-toh oon rreh-**see**-boh (Am) neh-theh-**see**-toh oon rreh-**thee**-boh (Sp)

BOOKSTORE OR NEWSSTAND

I would like...	*Quisiera...*	*kee-**syeh**-rah*
a newspaper	un periódico	oon pehr-**yoh**-dee-koh
some post cards	tarjetas postales	tahr-**heh**-tahs poh-**stah**-lehs
some English language magazines	revistas en inglés	rreh-**bee**-stahs ehn een-**glehs**
a city map	un mapa de la ciudad	oon **mah**-pah deh lah syoo-**dahd** (Am) oon **mah**-pah deh lah thyoo-**dahd** (Sp)

I would like...	*Quisiera...*	*kee-**syeh**-rah*
a Spanish/English dictionary	un diccionario español/inglés	oon deek-syoh-**nah**-ryoh eh-spah-**nyohl** een-**glehs** (Am) oon deek-thyoh-**nah**-ryoh eh-spah-**nyohl** een-**glehs** (Sp)
some stationery	papel de escribir	pah-**pehl** deh eh-skree-**beer**
some envelopes	sobres	**soh**-brehs
some stamps	timbres (Mexico) estampillas (Am) sellos (Sp)	**teem**-brehs (Mexico) eh-stahm-**pee**-yahs (Am) **seh**-lyohs (Sp)
some wrapping paper	papel de envolver	pah-**pehl** deh ehn-bohl-**behr**
some sticky tape	cinta adhesiva	**seen**-tah ah-deh-**see**-bah (Am) **theen**-tah ah-deh-**see**-bah(Sp)

CAMERA SHOP

I would like a roll of...	*Quisiera un rollo de...*	*kee-**syeh**-rah oon **rroh**-yoh deh (Am)* *kee-**syeh**-rah oon **rroh**-lyoh deh (Sp)*
film	película	peh-**lee**-koo-lah
print film	película para fotografías	peh-**lee**-koo-lah **pah**-rah foh-toh-grah-**fee**-ahs
slide film	película para diapositivas	peh-**lee**-koo-lah **pah**-rah dyah-poh-see-**tee**-bahs
I need batteries for my camera.	Necesito pilas para mi cámara	neh-seh-**see**-toh **pee**-lahs **pah**-rah mee **kah**-mah-rah (Am) neh-theh-**see**-toh **pee**-lahs **pah**-rah mee **kah**-mah-rah (Sp)
I'd like a cassette for my camcorder.	Quisiera una videocasete para mi cámara de vídeo	kee-**syeh**-rah **oo**-nah bee-deh-oh-kah-**seh**-teh **pah**-rah mee **kah**-mah-rah deh **bee**-deh-oh

Purchase your film before you leave so you can shop around for the best deal. You may also want to wait until your return to have your film developed. Film and developing in Spain, Mexico and Latin America can be extremely expensive.

JEWELLERY STORE

I'd like to see...	*Quisiera ver...*	*kee-**syeh**-rah behr*
a bracelet	una pulsera	**oo**-nah pool-**seh**-rah
a brooch	un broche	oon **broh**-cheh
a chain	una cadena	**oo**-nah kah-**deh**-nah
some earrings	unos aretes (Am)	**oo**-nohs ah-**reh**-tehs (Am)
	unos pendientes (Sp)	**oo**-nohs pehn-**dyehn**-tehs (Sp)
a necklace	un collar	oon koh-**yahr** (Am)
		oon koh-**lyahr** (Sp)
a ring	un anillo	oon ah-**nee**-yoh (Am)
		oon ah-**nee**-lyoh (Sp)
a watch	un reloj	oon rreh-**loh**
Do you have it in...?	*¿Lo tiene en...?*	*loh **tyeh**-neh ehn*
gold	oro	**oh**-roh
white gold	oro blanco	**oh**-roh **blahn**-koh
pink gold	oro rosado	**oh**-roh rroh-**sah**-doh
silver	plata	**plah**-tah

RECORDS, TAPES AND CDS

I'd like to buy...	*Quisiera comprar...*	*kee-**syeh**-rah kohm-**prahr***
a CD	un disco compacto	oon **dee**-skoh kohm-**pahk**-toh
a record	un disco	oon **dee**-skoh
a tape	una cinta	**oo**-nah **seen**-tah (Am)
		oo-nah **theen**-tah (Sp)

I like...music.	*Me gusta la música...*	*meh **goo**-stah lah **moo**-see-kah*
classical	clásica	**klah**-see-kah
popular	popular	poh-poo-**lahr**
Latin American	latina	lah-**tee**-nah
Spanish	española	eh-spah-**nyoh**-lah
rock	rocanrol	rroh-kahn-**rrohl**

BARGAINING

The following expressions will be useful when bargaining in the open-air and flea markets that abound in Mexico and Latin America. If you'd like to purchase an article, ask the price and then start to bargain. Offer between a half and two-thirds of the asking price. The merchant will probably make another offer. By going back and forth, you should reach a price that is reasonable for both of you. If the merchant doesn't seem willing to negotiate to your satisfaction, don't be afraid to say "no thank you" and then start to walk away. The merchant may call you back and negotiate a bit more. Bargaining can be stressful for people who aren't accustomed to it. However, it is expected in the markets and it can actually be a lot of fun. Once you've made your purchase, you can relax - just smile and thank the merchant before moving on. Remember that many flea markets accept credit cards.

How much does it cost?	¿Cuánto cuesta?	**kwahn**-toh **kweh**-stah
It's too much.	Es demasiado.	ehs deh-mah-**syah**-doh
I don't like it.	No me gusta.	noh meh **goo**-stah
I'll give you...	Le doy...	leh doy
No, thank you.	No, gracias.	noh **grah**-syahs (Am) noh **grah**-thyahs (Sp)
Would you take...?	¿Aceptaría...?	ah-sehp-tah-**ree**-ah (Am) ah-thehp-tah-**ree**-ah (Sp)
Thank you very much.	Muchas gracias.	**moo**-chahs **grah**-syahs (Am) **moo**-chahs **grah**-thyahs (Sp)
I'll take it.	Me lo llevo.	meh loh **yeh**-boh (Am) meh loh **lyeh**-boh (Sp)

SIGN LANGUAGE

CHILDREN'S DEPARTMENT	DEPARTAMENTO DE NIÑOS
ELECTRONICS DEPARTMENT	DEPARTAMENTO DE ELECTRÓNICA
HOUSEWARES	DEPARTAMENTO DEL HOGAR
JEWELLERY DEPARTMENT	JOYERÍA
MEN'S DEPARTMENT	DEPARTAMENTO DE CABALLEROS
PERFUME DEPARTMENT	PERFUMERÍA
SHOE DEPARTMENT	ZAPATERÍA
SPORTS DEPARTMENT	DEPARTAMENTO DE DEPORTES
WOMEN'S DEPARTMENT	DEPARTAMENTO DE SEÑORAS
YOUTH'S DEPARTMENT	DEPARTAMENTO DE JÓVENES
CASHIER	CAJA
ON SALE	EN OFERTA
OPEN	ABIERTO
CLOSED	CERRADO
UP	SUBIDA
DOWN	BAJADA
LADIES	DAMAS/SEÑORAS
GENTLEMEN	CABALLEROS
ELEVATOR	ASCENSOR
ESCALATOR	ESCALERA AUTOMÁTICA or ESCALERA ELÉCTRICA or ESCALERA MECÁNICA or ESCALERA MÓVIL or ESCALERA RODANTE

CHAPTER TEN

Phoning and faxing

Making phone calls in Spanish-speaking countries can sometimes be a frustrating experience for Canadian tourists. Phones are not always the state-of-the-art machines that we find in Canada. This is not to say that modern phones do not exist, but be prepared for some differences. The dial tone and the ring may be different than what you've come to expect. Some pay phones accept coins, tokens or a variety of credit and phone cards. If you find phoning difficult, you can always place calls through your hotel where the people at the reception desk will help you. However, if you wish to phone home, a calling card can save you a great deal of money. Call your long-distance carrier before you leave, explain that you are travelling abroad and make sure your long-distance calling card will work in Spain, Mexico or Latin America.

Here are some expressions that you will find useful:

Where is there a public phone?	¿Dónde hay un teléfono público?	**dohn**-deh ahy oon teh-**leh**-foh-noh **poo**-blee-koh
Do you have a phone directory?	¿Tiene un directorio de teléfonos? (Am)	**tyeh**-neh oon dee-rehk-**toh**-ryoh deh teh-**leh**-foh-nohs (Am)
	¿Tiene una guía telefónica? (Sp)	**tyeh**-neh **oo**-nah **gee**-ah teh-leh-**foh**-nee-kah (Sp)
Where is there a phone booth?	¿Dónde hay una caseta de teléfono? (Am)	**dohn**-deh ahy **oo**-nah kah-**seh**-tah deh teh-**leh**-foh-noh (Am)

Where is there a phone booth?	¿Dónde hay una cabina telefónica? (Sp)	**dohn**-deh ahy **oo**-nah kah-**bee**-nah teh-leh-**foh**-nee-kah (Sp)
I'd like to make a...call.	*Quisiera hacer una llamada...*	*kee-**syeh**-rah ah-**sehr** oo-nah yah-**mah**-dah (Am)* *kee-**syeh**-rah ah-**thehr** **oo**-nah lyah-**mah**-dah (Sp)*
local	local	loh-**kahl**
long-distance	de larga distancia	deh **lahr**-gah dee-**stahn**-syah (Am) deh **lahr**-gah dee-**stahn**-thyah (Sp)
person-to-person	de persona a persona	deh pehr-**soh**-nah ah pehr-**soh**-nah
collect	por cobrar	pohr koh-**brahr**
I'd like to make a phone call. Can you help me?	Quisiera hacer una llamada telefónica. ¿Puede ayudarme?	kee-**syeh**-rah ah-**sehr** **oo**-nah yah-**mah**-dah teh-leh-**foh**-nee-kah **pweh**-deh ah-yoo-**dahr**-meh (Am) kee-**syeh**-rah ah-**thehr** **oo**-nah lyah-**mah**-dah teh-leh-**foh**-nee-kah **pweh**-deh ah-yoo-**dahr**-meh (Sp)
Will you phone for me?	¿Quiere telefonear de mi parte?	**kyeh**-reh teh-leh-foh-neh-**ahr** deh mee **pahr**-teh
May I speak with...?	¿Puedo hablar con...?	**pweh**-doh ah-**blahr** kohn
Who is this?	¿Con quién hablo?	kohn kyehn **ah**-bloh
Speak louder, please.	Hable más fuerte, por favor.	**ah**-bleh mahs **fwehr**-teh pohr fah-**bohr**
Speak slower, please.	Hable más despacio, por favor.	**ah**-bleh mahs deh-**spah**-syoh pohr fah-**bohr** (Am) **ah**-bleh mahs deh-**spah**-thyoh pohr fah-**bohr** (Sp)
I got cut off.	Me han cortado.	meh ahn kohr-**tah**-doh

Can you try again, please?	¿Quisiera llamar otra vez, por favor?	kee-**syeh**-rah yah-**mahr** **oh**-trah behs pohr fah-**bohr** (Am) kee-**syeh**-rah lyah-**mahr** **oh**-trah behth pohr fah-**bohr** (Sp)
Can I call direct?	¿Es posible marcar directamente?	ehs poh-**see**-bleh mahr-**kahr** dee-rehk-tah-**mehn**-teh

"Hello" is expressed in a variety of ways when talking on the phone. When answering the phone, you would say **Diga** (**dee**-gah) in Spain. In Mexico, you would say **Bueno (bweh**-noh). In Colombia and other parts of Latin America, you would say **A ver** (ah behr) or **Aló** (ah-**loh**). When you're initiating the call, you would say **Oiga** (**oy**-gah) or **Aló** (ah-**loh**).

Sending a fax is a fast and reliable way of communicating with people. However, remember that the information that you send via fax is not confidential. Whoever is on the receiving end will be able to read your message. Your hotel staff will know where you can send a fax.

Here are some phrases that you'll need:

Where can I send a fax?	¿Dónde puedo enviar un fax?	**dohn**-deh **pweh**-doh ehm-**byahr** oon fahks
I'd like to send a fax.	Quisiera enviar un fax.	kee-**syeh**-rah ehm-**byahr** oon fahks
How much does it cost to send a fax?	¿Cuánto cuesta enviar un fax?	**kwahn**-toh **kweh**-stah ehm-**byahr** oon fahks
How much is it per page?	¿Cuánto cuesta por página?	**kwahn**-toh **kweh**-stah pohr **pah**-hee-nah

CHAPTER ELEVEN

Other services

AT THE PHARMACY (INCLUDING TOILETRIES)

I want to buy...	*Quiero comprar...*	***kyeh**-roh kohm-**prahr***
an antacid	un antiácido	oon ahn-**tyah**-see-doh (Am) oon ahn-**tyah**-thee-doh (Sp)
an antiseptic	un antiséptico	oon ahn-tee-**sehp**-tee-koh
aspirins	apirinas	ah-spee-**ree**-nahs
bandaids	curitas	koo-**ree**-tahs
a brush	un cepillo	oon seh-**pee**-yoh (Am) oon theh-**pee**-lyoh (Sp)
a comb	un peine	oon **pay**-neh
conditioner	suavizante	swah-bee-**sahn**-teh (Am) swah-bee-**thahn**-teh (Sp)
condoms	condones	kohn-**doh**-nehs
a package of condoms	un paquete de condones	oon pah-**keh**-teh deh kohn-**doh**-nehs
contact lens solution	solución limpiadora para lentes de contacto	soh-loo-**syohn** leem-pyah-**doh**-rah **pah**-rah **lehn**-tehs deh kohn-**tahk**-toh (Am) soh-loo-**thyohn** leem-pyah-**doh**-rah **pah**-rah **lehn**-tehs deh kohn-**tahk**-toh (Sp)
cough syrup	jarabe para la tos	hah-**rah**-beh **pah**-rah lah tohs
dental floss	seda dental	**seh**-dah dehn-**tahl**
a deodorant	un desodorante	oon deh-soh-doh-**rahn**-teh
emery boards	limas de cartón	**lee**-mahs deh kahr-**tohn**

facial tissues	pañuelos de papel	pah-**nyweh**-lohs deh pah-**pehl**
hairspray	laca	**lah**-kah
insect repellant	repelente	rreh-peh-**lehn**-teh
a laxative	un laxante	oon lahk-**sahn**-teh
milk of magnesia	leche de magnesia	**leh**-cheh deh mahg-**neh**-syah
mouthwash	antiséptico bucal	ahn-tee-**sehp**-tee-koh boo-**kahl**
nail clippers	un cortauñas	oon kohr-tah-**oo**-nyahs
a nail file	una lima de uñas	**oo**-nah **lee**-mah deh **oo**-nyahs
nose drops	gotas para la nariz	**goh**-tahs **pah**-rah lah nah-**rees** (Am) **goh**-tahs **pah**-rah lah nah-**reeth** (Sp)
a razor	una navaja	**oo**-nah nah-**bah**-hah
razor blades	hojas de afeitar	**oh**-hahs deh ah-fay-**tahr**
safety pins	imperdibles	eem-pehr-**dee**-blehs
sanitary napkins	toallas sanitarias	toh-**ah**-yahs sah-nee-**tah**-ryahs (Am) toh-**ah**-lyahs sah-nee-**tah**-ryahs (Sp)
scissors	tijeras	tee-**heh**-rahs
shampoo	champú	chahm-**poo**
shaving cream	crema de afeitar	**kreh**-mah deh ah-fay-**tahr**
some soap	jabón	hah-**bohn**
sun block	loción protectora	loh-**syohn** proh-tehk-**toh**-rah (Am) loh-**thyohn** proh-tehk-**toh**-rah (Sp)
suntan lotion	loción bronceadora	loh-**syohn** brohn-seh-ah-**doh**-rah (Am) loh-**thyohn** brohn-theh-ah-**doh**-rah (Sp)
suppositories	supositorios	soo-poh-see-**toh**-ryohs
tampons	tampones	tahm-**poh**-nehs

a toothbrush	un cepillo de dientes	oon seh-**pee**-yoh deh **dyehn**-tehs (Am)
		oon theh-**pee**-lyoh deh **dyehn**-tehs (Sp)
toothpaste	pasta de dientes	**pah**-stah deh **dyehn**-tehs

AT THE LAUNDRY AND DRY CLEANERS

Where is there...?	*¿Dónde hay...?*	***dohn**-deh ahy*
a laundry	una lavandería	**oo**-nah lah-bahn-deh-**ree**-ah
a dry cleaner's shop	una tintorería	**oo**-nah teen-toh-reh-**ree**-ah
a laundromat	una lavandería automática	**oo**-nah lah-bahn-deh-**ree**-ah ow-toh-**mah**-tee-kah
I want this...	*Quiero que me lo...*	***kyeh**-roh keh meh loh*
washed	laven	**lah**-behn
dry cleaned	limpien en seco	**leem**-pyehn ehn **seh**-koh
ironed (pressed)	planchen	**plahn**-chehn
mended	arreglen	ah-**rreh**-glehn
There's a button missing.	Falta un botón.	**fahl**-tah oon boh-**tohn**
Can you sew it on please?	¿Puede coserlo, por favor?	**pweh**-deh koh-**sehr**-loh pohr fah-**bohr**
Can you fix the zipper?	¿Puede arreglar el cierre relámpago? (Am)	**pweh**-deh ah-rreh-**glahr** ehl **syeh**-rreh rreh-**lahm**-pah-goh (Am)
	¿Puede arreglar la cremallera? (Sp)	**pweh**-deh ah-rreh-**glahr** lah kreh-mah-**lyeh**-rah (Sp)

AT THE BARBERSHOP AND HAIR SALON

Where's the nearest barbershop?	¿Dónde está la barbería más cercana?	**dohn**-deh eh-**stah** lah bahr-beh-**ree**-ah mahs sehr-**kah**-nah (Am)
		dohn-deh eh-**stah** lah bahr-beh-**ree**-ah mahs thehr-**kah**-nah (Sp)
Where's the nearest hair salon?	¿Dónde está la peluquería más cercana?	**dohn**-deh eh-**stah** lah peh-loo-keh-**ree**-ah mahs sehr-**kah**-nah (Am)

Where's the nearest hair salon?	¿Dónde está la peluquería más cercana?	**dohn**-deh eh-**stah** lah peh-loo-keh-**ree**-ah mahs thehr-**kah**-nah (Sp)
I'd like...	*Quisiera...*	*kee-**syeh**-rah*
a haircut	un corte de pelo	oon **kohr**-teh deh **peh**-loh
a wash, cut and set	un lavado, un corte y un peinado	oon lah-**bah**-doh oon **kohr**-teh ee oon pay-**nah**-doh
a blow dry	un modelado	oon moh-deh-**lah**-doh
Not too short.	No muy corto.	noh mwee **kohr**-toh
I want it short.	Quiero el pelo corto.	**kyeh**-roh ehl **peh**-loh **kohr**-toh
I want it long.	Lo quiero largo.	loh **kyeh**-roh **lahr**-goh
How much is it?	¿Cuánto es?	**kwahn**-toh ehs
Is the service included?	¿Está incluida la propina?	eh-**stah** een-**klwee**-dah lah proh-**pee**-nah

AT THE POST OFFICE

Where's the nearest post office?	¿Dónde está la oficina de correos más cercana?	**dohn**-deh eh-**stah** lah oh-fee-**see**-nah deh koh-**rreh**-ohs mahs sehr-**kah**-nah (Am) **dohn**-deh eh-**stah** lah oh-fee-**thee**-nah deh koh-**rreh**-ohs mahs thehr-**kah**-nah (Am)
I'd like to send...	*Quiero mandar...*	***kyeh**-roh mahn-**dahr***
to Canada.	*a Canadá.*	*... ah kah-nah-**dah***
this letter	esta carta	**eh**-stah **kahr**-tah
this package	este paquete	**eh**-steh pah-**keh**-teh
these postcards	estas tarjetas postales	**eh**-stahs tahr-**heh**-tahs poh-**stah**-lehs
How many stamps does it take?	¿Cuántos timbres lleva? (Mexico)	**kwahn**-tohs **teem**-brehs **yeh**-bah (Mexico)
	¿Cuántas estampillas lleva? (Am)	**kwahn**-tahs eh-stahm-**pee**-yahs **yeh**-bah (Am)
	¿Cuántos sellos lleva? (Sp)	**kwahn**-tohs **seh**-lyohs **lyeh**-bah (Sp)

I want to insure this.	Quiero asegurar esto.	**kyeh**-roh ah-seh-goo-**rahr** **eh**-stoh
How much is the insurance?	¿Cuánto cuesta el seguro?	**kwahn**-toh **kweh**-stah ehl seh-**goo**-roh
I'd like a receipt.	Quisiera un recibo.	kee-**syeh**-rah oon rreh-**see**-boh (Am) kee-**syeh**-rah oon rreh-**thee**-boh (Sp)

An ounce of prevention...

Tourists are often victims of crime in major cities around the world. Be prepared. Never walk around with large sums of cash in your pockets. Keep most of your money and your traveller's cheques at the hotel. Always keep a separate list of the numbers of your traveller's cheques. Men should never keep wallets in inside coat pockets or the back pockets of pants. Women should carry purses or knapsacks that are closed and held close to the body. That group of friendly locals who surround you to talk may end up with your wallet while you're still thumbing through this phrase book. If that happens, shout...

Help me!	¡Ayúdeme!	ah-**yoo**-deh-meh
I need a policeman!	¡Necesito un policía!	neh-seh-**see**-toh oon poh-lee-**see**-ah (Am) neh-theh-**see**-toh oon poh-lee-**thee**-ah (Sp)
Someone stole my wallet.	Me ha robado mi cartera.	meh ah rroh-**bah**-doh mee kahr-**teh**-rah

CHAPTER TWELVE

Medical and emergency phrases

Peace of mind is very important when you're travelling. Knowing that you are covered for medical emergencies can remove a lot of the uncertainty and fear that people experience when travelling to foreign countries. You may already be covered for doctors' and emergency hospital visits through your employment. However, some of these plans will require you to pay for medical services that you receive in Spain or Latin America "up front." With these plans, it's only upon your return that you make a claim to your hospital plan for reimbursement. Getting ill while abroad can be very costly, especially if you're not adequately covered.

There are many insurance packages available for tourists that will cover your medical emergencies while outside Canada. Very often, these plans will include a 24-hour, toll-free number that you can use to access the medical attention that you require. Some of these plans will even recommend certain doctors and will direct you to the nearest hospital that will deal with your emergency situation. The plan will arrange for payment so that you won't be "out of pocket" for the services that you receive. Your travel agent or the automobile association will offer you this type of insurance that is sure to meet your needs.

This chapter will equip you with the necessary phrases to deal with emergency situations requiring a doctor, a dentist, an eye-care specialist, as well as the police. Remember to keep your insurance policy and the toll-free number with you at all times so that you're prepared to deal with emergencies when and if they arise. Fill out the Emergency Card at the end of this chapter so that you'll have all of your personal information at hand.

EMERGENCIES REQUIRING A DOCTOR

Help!	¡Socorro!	soh-**koh**-rroh
I need a doctor.	Necesito un médico.	neh-seh-**see**-toh oom **meh**-dee-koh (Am) neh-theh-**see**-toh oom **meh**-dee-koh (Sp)
Send for a doctor!	¡Manden por un médico!	**mahn**-dehn pohr oom **meh**-dee-koh
Send for an ambulance immediately!	¡Manden por una ambulancia en seguida!	**mahn**-dehn pohr **oo**-nah ahm-boo-**lahn**-syah ehn seh-**gee**-dah (Am) **mahn**-dehn pohr **oo**-nah ahm-boo-**lahn**-thyah ehn seh-**gee**-dah (Sp)
Call the police!	¡Llamen a la policía!	**yah**-mehn ah lah poh-lee-**see**-ah (Am) **lyah**-mehn ah lah poh-lee-**thee**-ah (Sp)
Do you know a doctor who speaks English?	¿Conoce un médico que hable inglés?	koh-**noh**-seh oon **meh**-dee-koh keh **ah**-bleh een-**glehs** (Am) koh-**noh**-theh oom **meh**-dee-koh keh **ah**-bleh een-**glehs** (Sp)

Explaining your symptoms

I don't feel well.	No me siento bien.	noh meh **syehn**-toh byehn
I'm sick.	Estoy enfermo (a).	eh-**stoy** ehn-**fehr**-moh(mah)
I'm constipated.	Estoy estreñido (a).	eh-**stoy** eh-streh-**nyee**-doh(dah)
I have...	*Tengo...*	***tehn**-goh*
a broken bone	una fractura	**oo**-nah frahk-**too**-rah
a bruise	una contusión	**oo**-nah kohn-too-**syohn**
a burn	una quemadura	**oo**-nah keh-mah-**doo**-rah
a cold	un resfrío (Am) un resfriado (Sp)	oon rrehs-**free**-oh (Am) oon rrehs-**fryah**-doh (Sp)
a cough	una tos	**oo**-nah tohs
cramps	calambres	kah-**lahm**-brehs
a cut	una cortada	**oo**-nah kohr-**tah**-dah

diarrhea	diarrea	dyah-**rreh**-ah
a fever	una fiebre	**oo**-nah **fyeh**-breh
the flu	la gripe	lah **gree**-peh
a headache	un dolor de cabeza	oon doh-**lohr** deh kah-**beh**-sah (Am) oon doh-**lohr** deh kah-**beh**-thah (Sp)
heartburn	acidez del estómago	ah-see-**dehs** dehl eh-**stoh**-mah-goh (Am) ah-thee-**dehth** dehl eh-**stoh**-mah-goh (Sp)
indigestion	indigestión	een-dee-hehs-**tyohn**
an infection	una infección	**oo**-nah een-fehk-**syohn** (Am) **oo**-nah een-fehk-**thyohn** (Sp)
an itch	una sarna	**oo**-nah **sahr**-nah
a lump	un bulto	oon **bool**-toh
nausea	náuseas	**now**-seh-ahs
a rash	una erupción	**oo**-nah eh-roop-**syohn** (Am) **oo**-nah eh-roop-**thyohn** (Sp)
a sore throat	inflamación de la garanta	een-flah-mah-**syohn** deh lah gahr-**gahn**-tah (Am) een-flah-mah-**thyohn** de lah gahr-**gahn**-tah (Sp)
a stomach ache	un dolor del estómago	oon doh-**lohr** dehl eh-**stoh**-mah-goh
a swelling	una inflamación	**oo**-nah een-flah-mah-**syohn** (Am) **oo**-nah een-flah-mah-**thyohn** (Sp)
a sunburn	una quemadura del sol	**oo**-nah keh-mah-**doo**-rah dehl sohl.
a wound	un herido	oon eh-**ree**-doh

To indicate that a single part of your body hurts you, you would begin with **Me duele....** If more than one thing aches, you begin with **Me duelen....**

My...hurts.	*Me duele...*	*meh **dweh**-leh*
ankle	el tobillo	ehl toh-**bee**-yoh (Am)
		ehl toh-**bee**-lyoh (Sp)
arm	el brazo	ehl **brah**-soh (Am)
		ehl **brah**-thoh (Sp)
back	la espalda	lah eh-**spahl**-dah
breast/chest	el pecho	ehl **peh**-choh
ear	el oído	ehl oh-**ee**-doh
elbow	el codo	ehl **koh**-doh
eye	el ojo	eh **oh**-hoh
finger	el dedo	ehl **deh**-doh
foot	el pie	ehl pyeh
hand	la mano	lah **mah**-noh
head	la cabeza	lah kah-**beh**-sah (Am)
		lah kah-**beh**-thah (Sp)
knee	la rodilla	lah rroh-**dee**-yah (Am)
		lah rroh-**dee**-lyah (Sp)
leg	la pierna	lah **pyehr**-nah
neck	el cuello	ehl **kweh**-yoh (Am)
		ehl **kweh**-lyoh (Sp)
shoulder	el hombro	ehl **ohm**-broh
stomach	el estómago	ehl eh-**stoh**-mah-goh
throat	la garganta	lah gahr-**gahn**-tah
toe	el dedo del pie	ehl **deh**-doh dehl pyeh
tongue	la lengua	lah **lehn**-gwah
wrist	la muñeca	lah moo-**nyeh**-kah
My...hurt.	*Me duelen...*	*meh **dweh**-lehn*
buttocks	las nalgas	lahs **nahl**-gahs
eyes	los ojos	lohs **oh**-hohs
glands	las glándulas	lahs **glahn**-doo-lahs
muscles	los músculos	lohs **moo**-skoo-lohs
ribs	las costillas	lahs koh-**stee**-yahs (Am)
		lahs koh-**stee**-lyahs (Sp)
testicles	los testículos	lohs teh-**stee**-koo-lohs

I'm allergic to...	*Soy alérgico (a) a...*	*soy ah-**lehr**-hee-koh (kah) ah*
penicillin	la penicilina	lah peh-nee-see-**lee**-nah (Am) lah peh-nee-thee-**lee**-nah (Sp)
sulfa	la sulfa	la **sool**-fah
I'm pregnant.	Estoy embarazada.	eh-**stoy** ehm-bah-rah-**sah**-dah (Am) eh-**stoy** ehm-bah-rah-**thah**-dah (Sp)
I have menstrual cramps.	Tengo dolores menstruales.	**tehn**-goh doh-**loh**-rehs mehn-**strwah**-lehs
I have a chest pain.	Tengo dolor en el pecho.	**tehn**-goh doh-**lohr** ehn ehl **peh**-choh
I think I'm having a heart attack.	Creo que estoy teniendo un ataque cardíaco.	**kreh**-oh keh eh-**stoy** teh-**nyehn**-doh oon ah-**tah**-keh kahr-**dee**-ah-koh
I had a heart attack in (year).	Tuve un infarto en...	**too**-beh oon een-**fahr**-toh ehn
Can you give me a prescription?	¿Puede darme una receta?	**pweh**-deh **dahr**-meh **oo**-nah rreh-**seh**-tah (Am) **pweh**-deh **dahr**-meh **oo**-nah rreh-**theh**-tah (Sp)
Can you give me a receipt for my insurance?	¿Puede darme un recibo para mi seguro?	**pweh**-deh **dahr**-meh oon rreh-**see**-boh **pah**-rah mee seh-**goo**-roh (Am) **pweh**-deh **dahr**-meh oon rreh-**thee**-boh **pah**-rah mee seh-**goo**-roh (Sp)
Thank you very much, doctor.	Muchas gracias, doctor.	**moo**-chahs **grah**-syahs dohk-**tohr** (Am) **moo**-chahs **grah**-thyahs dohk-**tohr** (Sp)

EMERGENCIES REQUIRING A DENTIST

English	Spanish	Pronunciation
I need a dentist.	Necesito un dentista.	neh-seh-**see**-toh oon dehn-**tee**-stah (Am) neh-theh-**see**-toh oon dehn-**tee**-stah (Sp)
Do you know a dentist who speaks English?	¿Conoce un dentista que hable inglés?	koh-**noh**-seh oon dehn-**tee**-stah keh **ah**-bleh een-**glehs** (Am) koh-**noh**-theh oon dehn-**tee**-stah keh **ah**-bleh een-**glehs** (Sp)

Explaining your symptoms

English	Spanish	Pronunciation
Can you recommend a dentist?	¿Puede recomendar un dentista?	**pweh**-deh rreh-koh-mehn-**dahr** oon dehn-**tee**-stah
I broke my tooth.	Me rompí un diente.	meh rrohm-**pee** oon **dyehn**-teh
I lost a filling.	Perdí un arreglo.	pehr-**dee** oon ah-**rreh**-gloh
Can you fill it?	¿Puede empastarlo?	**pweh**-deh ehm-pah-**stahr**-loh
Can you give me a temporary filling?	¿Puede hacerme un empaste provisional?	**pweh**-deh ah-**sehr**-meh oon ehm-**pah**-steh proh-bee-syoh-**nahl** (Am) **pweh**-deh ah-**thehr**-meh oon ehm-**pah**-steh proh-bee-syoh-**nahl** (Sp)
My tooth hurts.	Me duele el diente.	meh **dweh**-leh ehl **dyehn**-teh
My gums are sore.	Me duelen las encías.	meh **dweh**-lehn lahs ehn-**see**-ahs (Am) meh **dweh**-lehn lahs ehn-**thee**-ahs (Sp)
I broke my denture.	Me rompí la dentadura.	meh rrohm-**pee** lah dehn-tah-**doo**-rah
Can you fix it?	¿Puede arreglarla?	**pweh**-deh ah-rreh-**glahr**-lah

How much do I owe you?	¿Cuánto le debo?	**kwahn**-toh leh **deh**-boh
Can you give me a receipt for my insurance?	¿Puede darme un recibo para mi seguro?	**pweh**-deh **dahr**-meh oon rreh-**see**-boh **pah**-rah mee seh-**goo**-roh (Am) **pweh**-deh **dahr**-meh oon rreh-**thee**-boh **pah**-rah mee seh-**goo**-roh (Sp)

EMERGENCIES REQUIRING AN EYE-CARE SPECIALIST

I broke...	*Rompí...*	*rrohm-**pee***
my glasses	las lentes (Am) las gafas (Sp)	lahs **lehn**-tehs (Am) lahs **gah**-fahs (Sp)
my frame	la montura	lah mohn-**too**-rah
my lens	un cristal	oon kree-**stahl**
I lost a contact lens.	Perdí una lente de contacto.	pehr-**dee** **oo**-nah **lehn**-teh deh kohn-**tahk**-toh
Can you replace it?	¿Puede reemplazarlo?	**pweh**-deh rrehm-plah-**sahr**-loh (Am) **pweh**-deh rrehm-plah-**thahr**-loh (Sp)

If your credit cards are stolen, cancel them immediately by phone. If your passport is lost or stolen or if you are detained by the police, immediately contact the Canadian Embassy or Consulate.

EMERGENCIES REQUIRING THE POLICE

The police should always be contacted if you've been attacked, been involved in a car accident or any accident involving injuries, and when thefts have occurred.

Call the police!	¡Llamen a la policía!	**yah**-mehn ah lah poh-lee-**see**-ah (Am) **lyah**-mehn ah lah poh-lee-**thee**-ah (Sp)
I need a policeman!	¡Necesito un policía!	neh-seh-**see**-toh oom poh-lee-**see**-ah (Am) neh-theh-**see**-toh oom poh-lee-**thee**-ah (Sp)
I'm going to call a policeman.	Voy a llamar un policía.	boy ah yah-**mahr** oom poh-lee-**see**-ah (Am) boy ah lyah-**mahr** oom poh-lee-**thee**-ah (Sp)
Where's the police station?	¿Dónde está la estación de policía?	**dohn**-deh eh-**stah** lah eh-stah-**syohn** deh poh-lee-**see**-ah (Am) **dohn**-deh eh-**stah** lah eh-stah-**thyohn** deh poh-lee-**thee**-ah (Sp)
It's an emergency!	¡Es una emergencia!	ehs **oo**-nah eh-mehr-**hehn**-syah (Am) ehs **oo**-nah eh-mehr-**hehn**-thyah (Sp)

I lost...	*Perdí...*	*pehr-**dee***
or		
Someone stole...	*Me ha robado...*	*meh ah rroh-**bah**-doh*
my credit cards	mis tarjetas de crédito	mees tahr-**heh**-tahs deh **kreh**-dee-toh
my identification	mi identificación	mee ee-dehn-tee-fee-kah-**syohn** (Am) mee ee-dehn-tee-fee-kah-**thyohn** (Sp)
my money	mi dinero	mee dee-**neh**-roh
my passport	mi pasaporte	mee pah-sah-**pohr**-teh
my purse	mi bolsa	mee **bohl**-sah

I lost...	*Perdí...*	*pehr-**dee***
or		
Someone stole...	*Me ha robado...*	*meh ah rroh-**bah**-doh*
my traveller's cheques	mis cheques de viajero	mees **cheh**-kehs deh byah-**heh**-roh
my wallet	mi cartera	mee kahr-**teh**-rah
I've been attacked.	Me ha atacado.	meh ah ah-tah-**kah**-doh
I prefer to talk to a woman.	Prefiero hablar con una mujer.	preh-**fyeh**-roh ah-**blahr** kohn **oo**-nah moo-**hehr**
Stop! Thief!	¡Socorro! ¡Ladrón!	soh-**koh**-rroh lah-**drohn**

We hope that you never have to use the phrases located in this section of your guide and phrase book. Be aware that they're here, at the end of the guide, in case you need to access them quickly.

Remember to fill out the Emergency Card on the following page of this guide so that you'll have all of your pertinent information at hand.

Emergency Card

Name: ____________________

Address: ____________________

Telephone number: ____________________

Blood group: ____________________

Health card number: ____________________

Medical insurance company
and policy number: ____________________

24-hour toll-free number: ____________________

Traveller's insurance company
and policy number: ____________________

Allergies: ____________________

Inoculations: ____________________

Person to contact in case of emergency:

Name: ____________________

Address: ____________________

Phone number: ____________________

NOTES & UPDATES

NOTES & UPDATES

NOTES & UPDATES

How to . . .

get the most from your
COLES NOTES

Key Point

Basic concepts in point form.

Close Up

Additional hints, notes, tips or background information.

Watch Out!

Areas where problems frequently occur.

Quick Tip

Concise ideas to help you learn what you need to know.

Remember This!

Essential material for mastery of the topic.